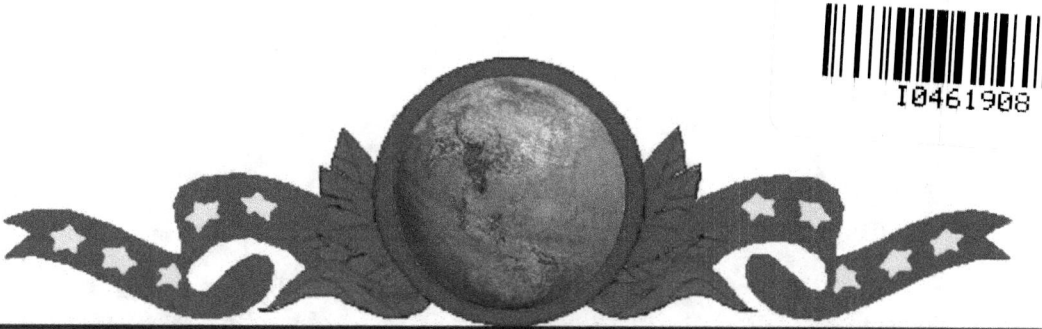

Real World
Colouring Book
For Advanced Users & Adults

Copyright 2019 By John Boom

50 Images

Created From Real Life Photos
For You To Colour As You Please.

ISBN 978-0-359-97232-6

9 780359 972326

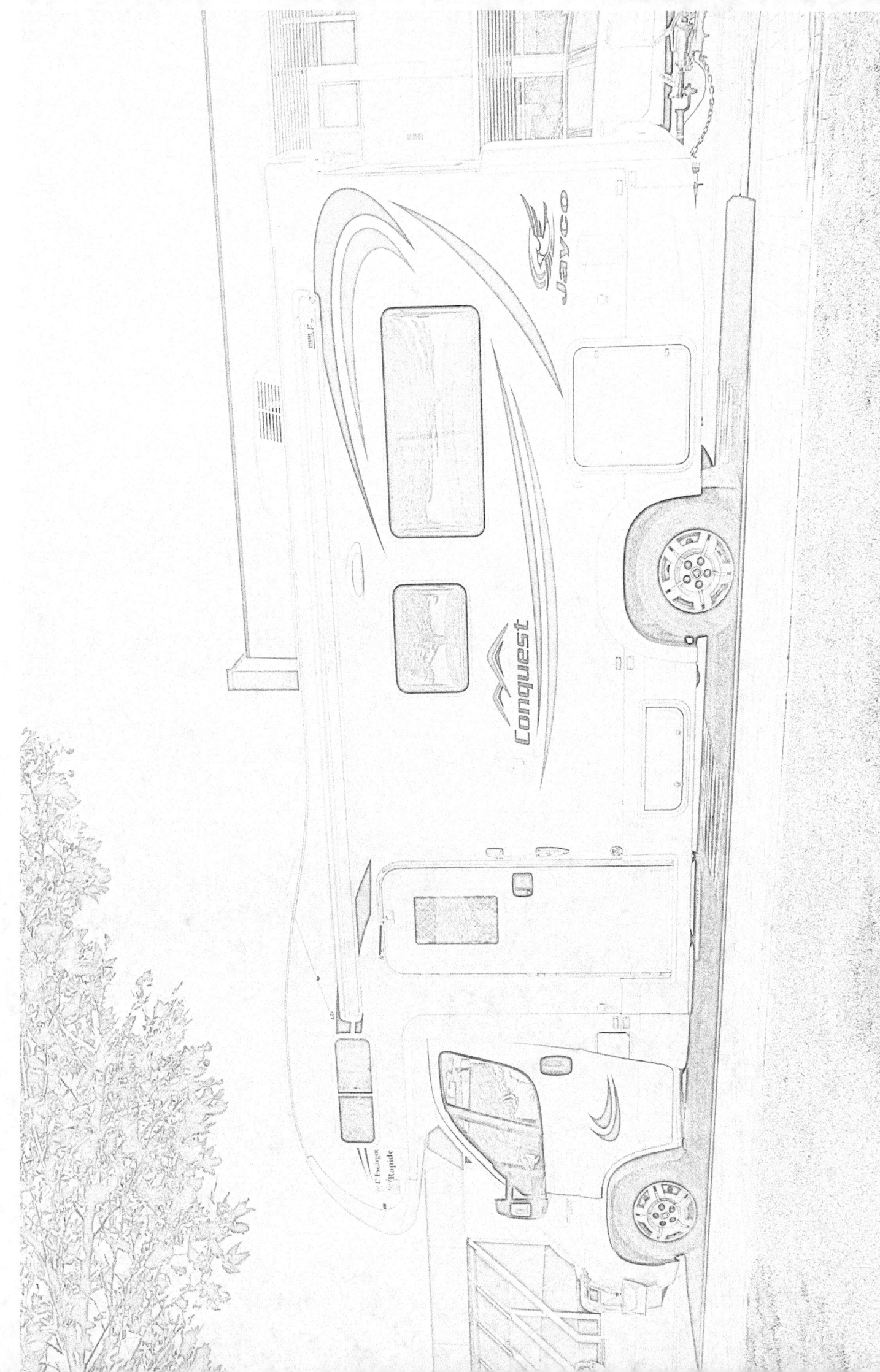

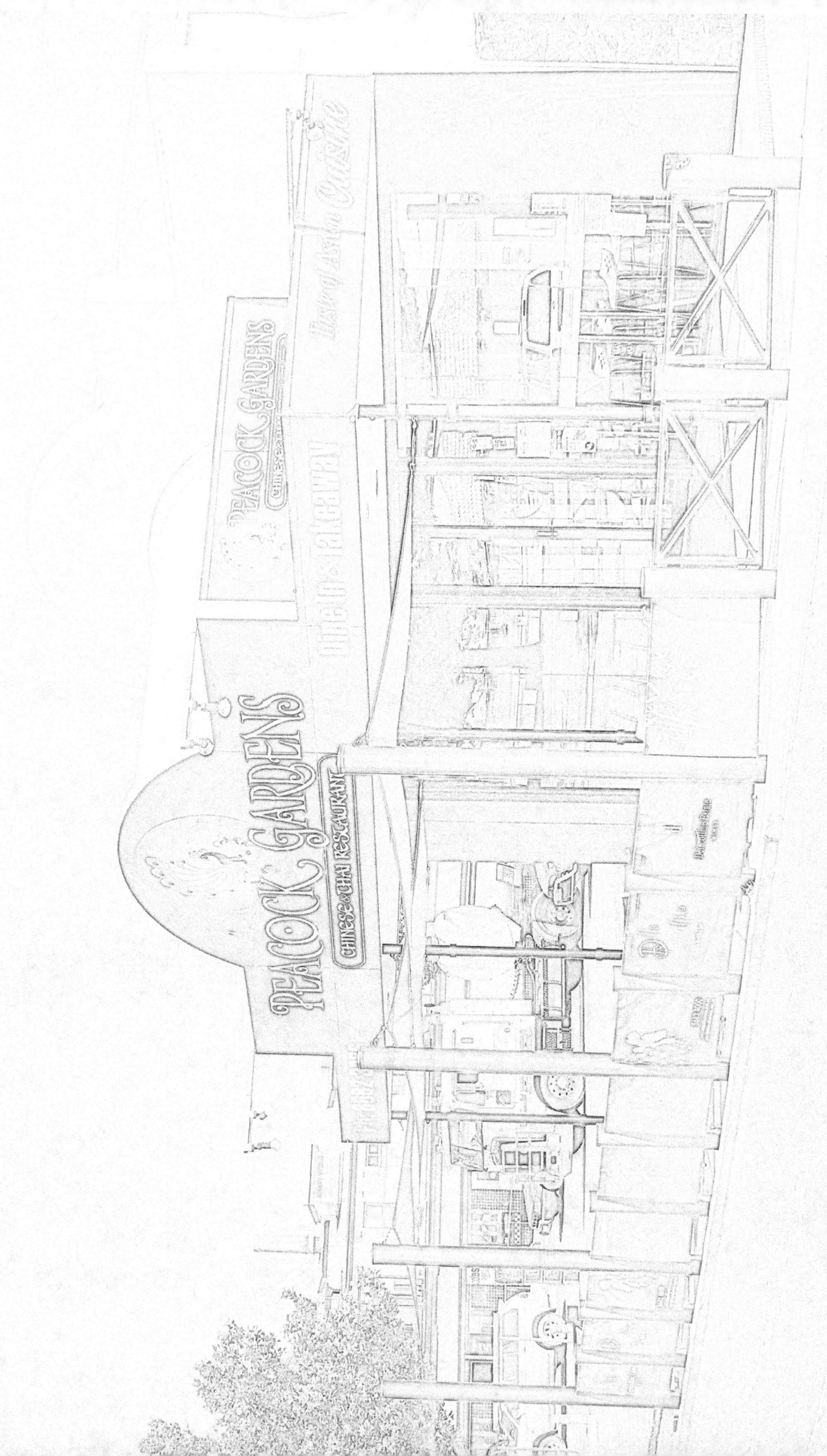

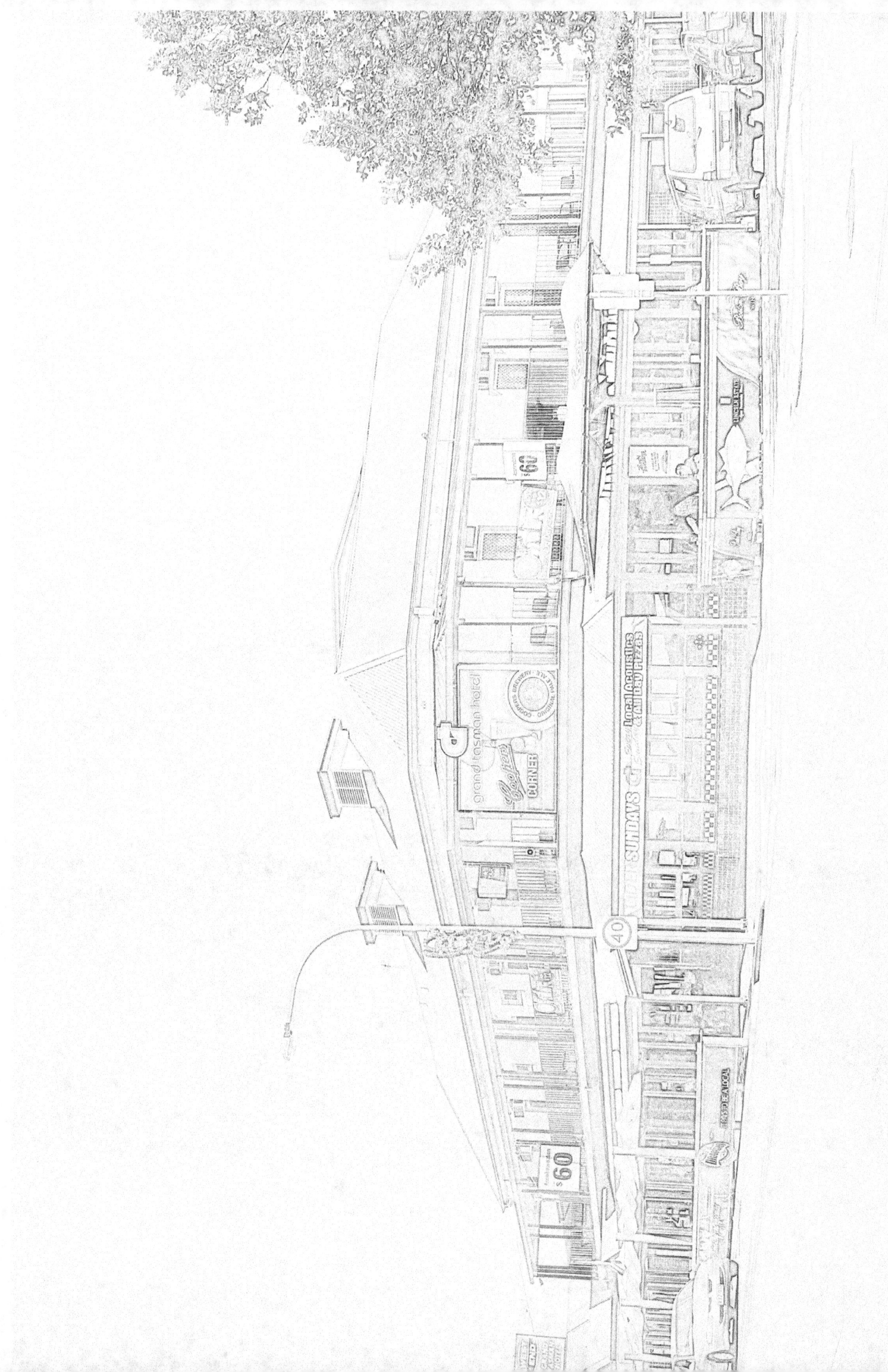

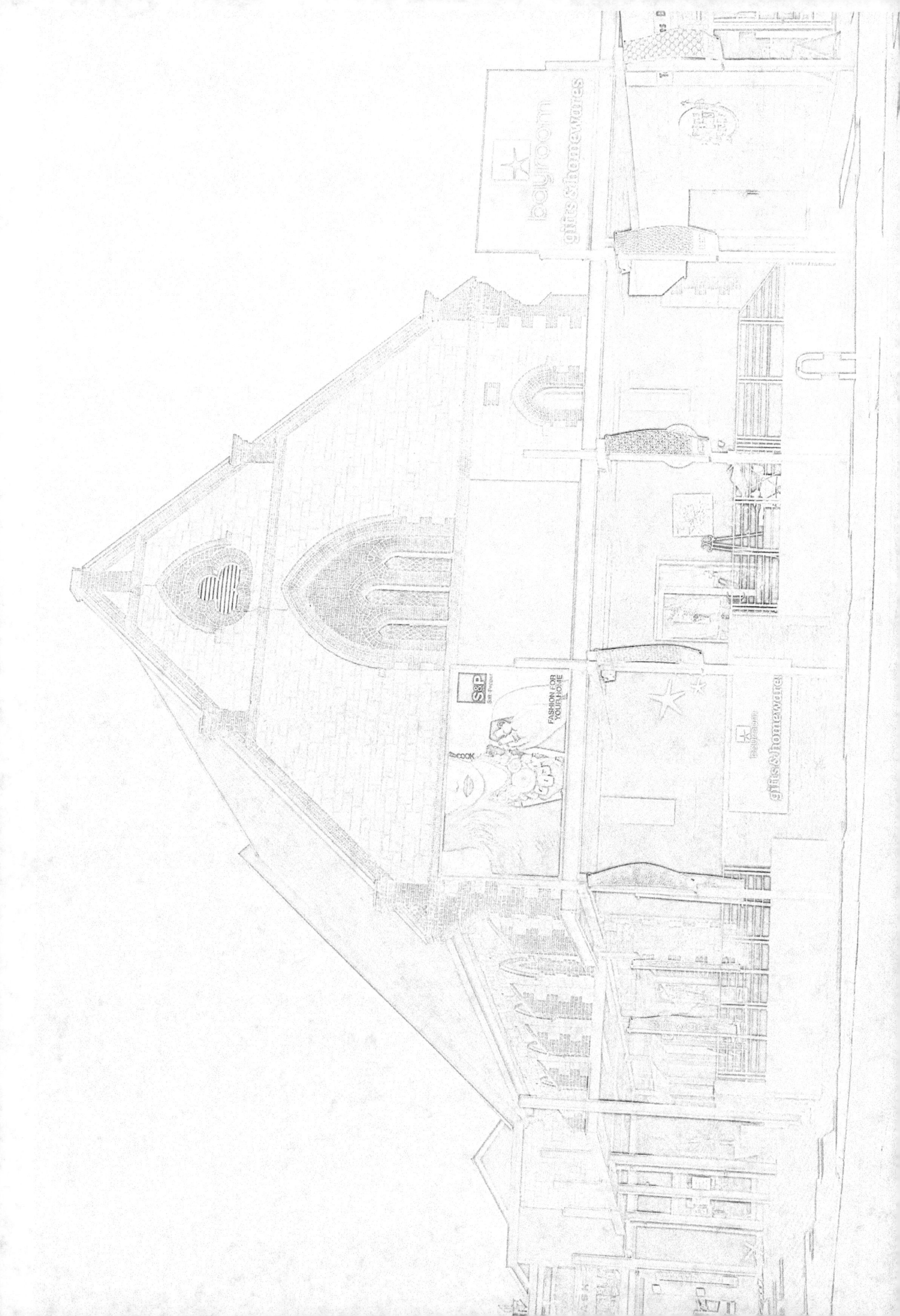

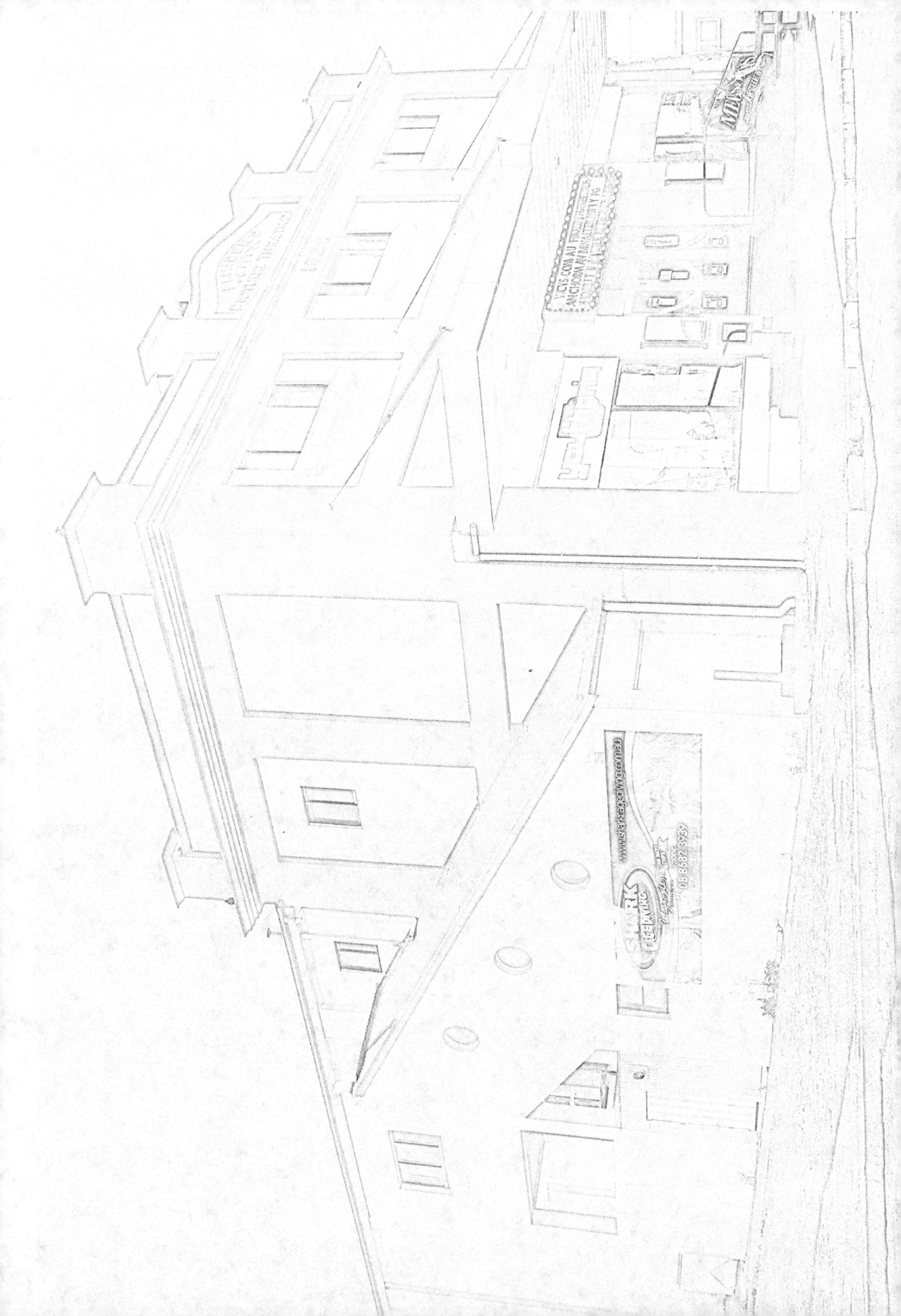

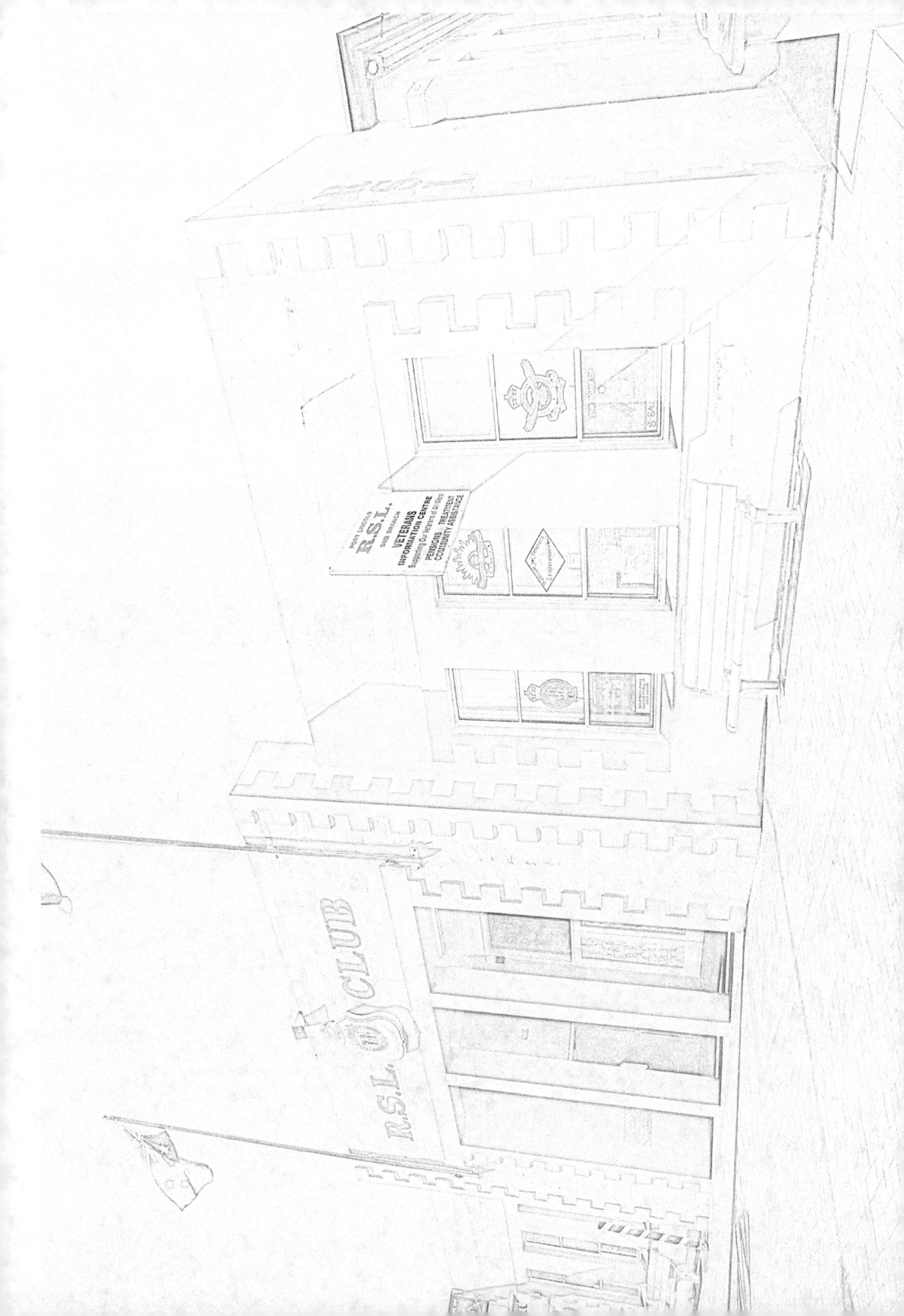

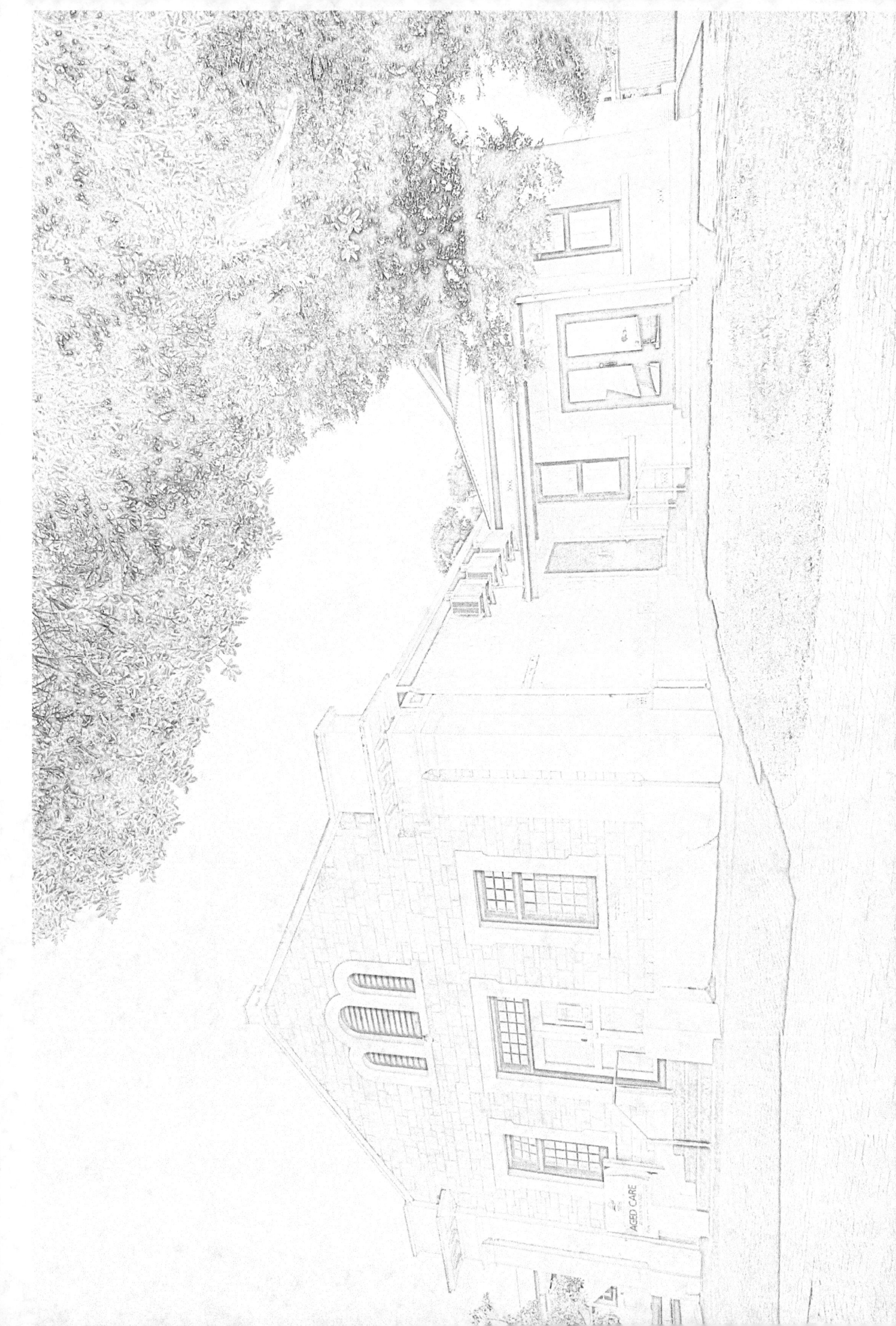

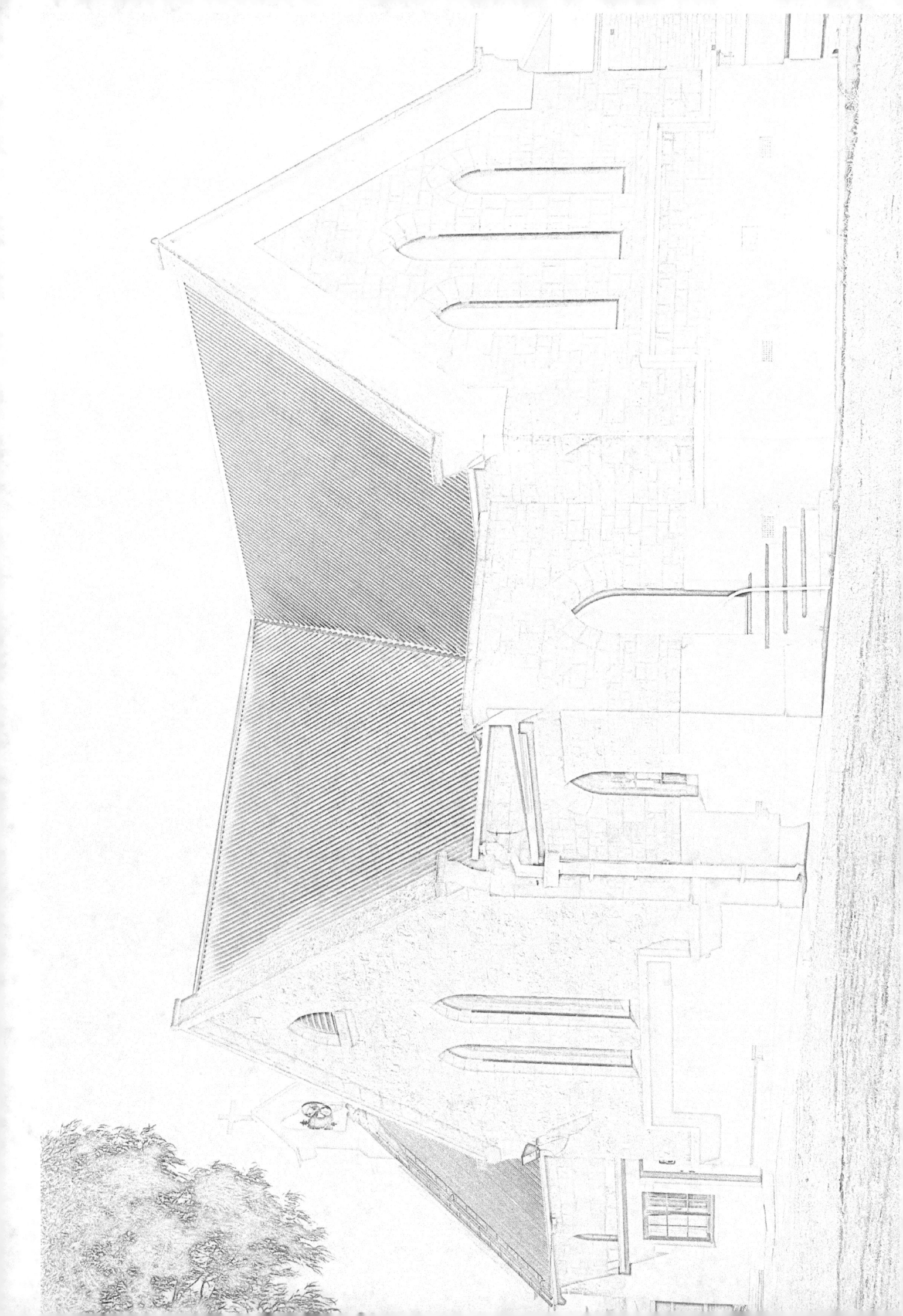

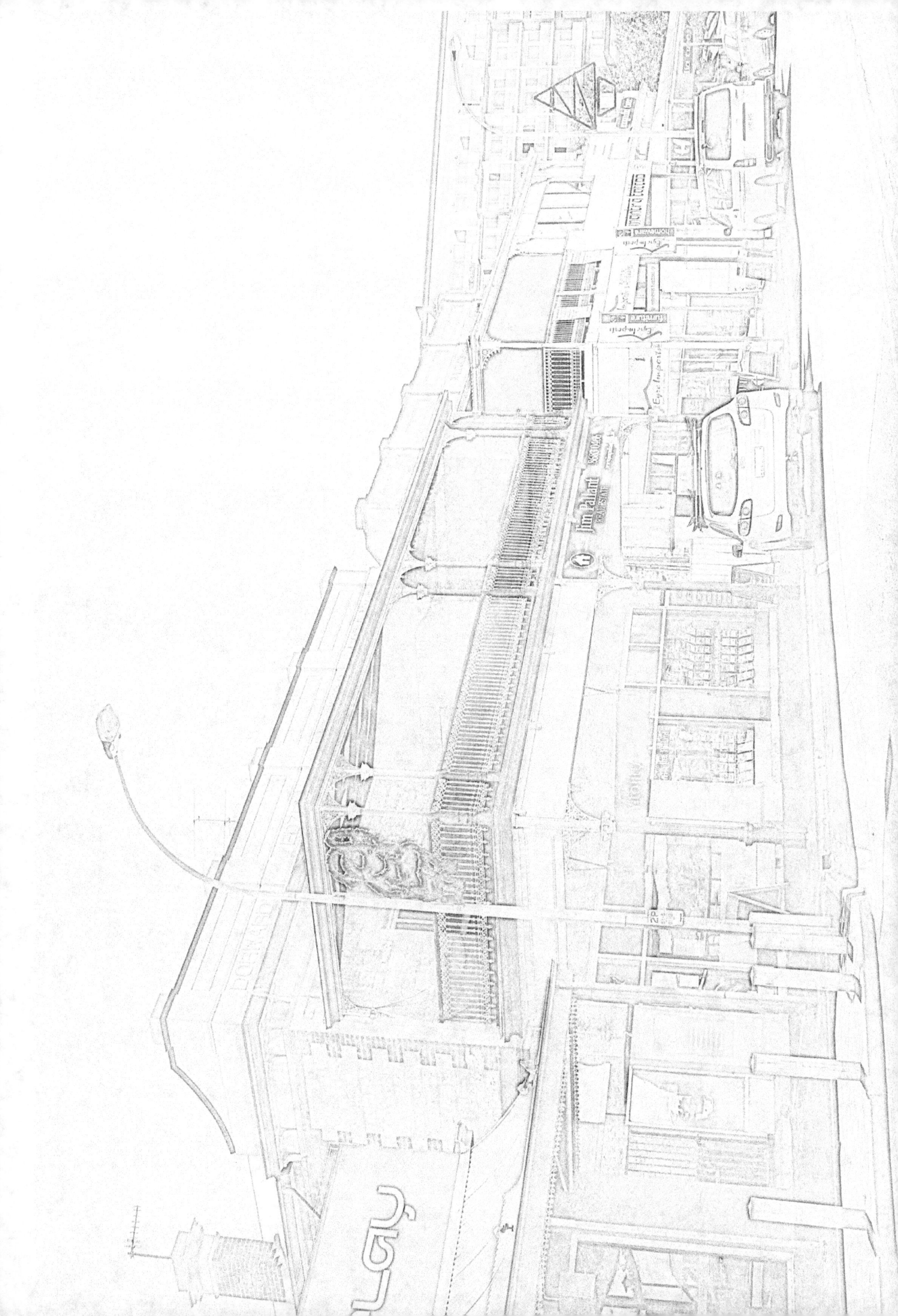

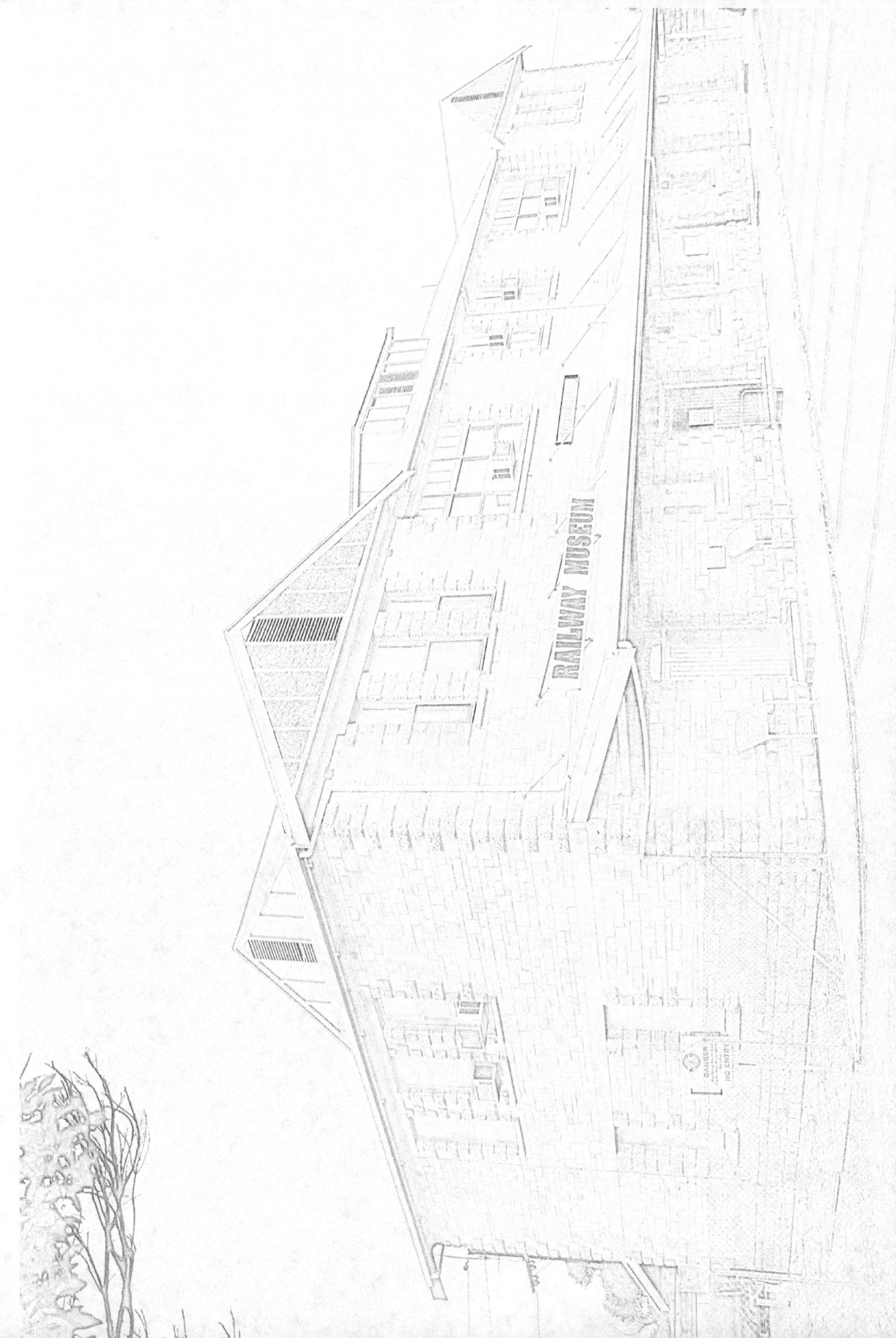

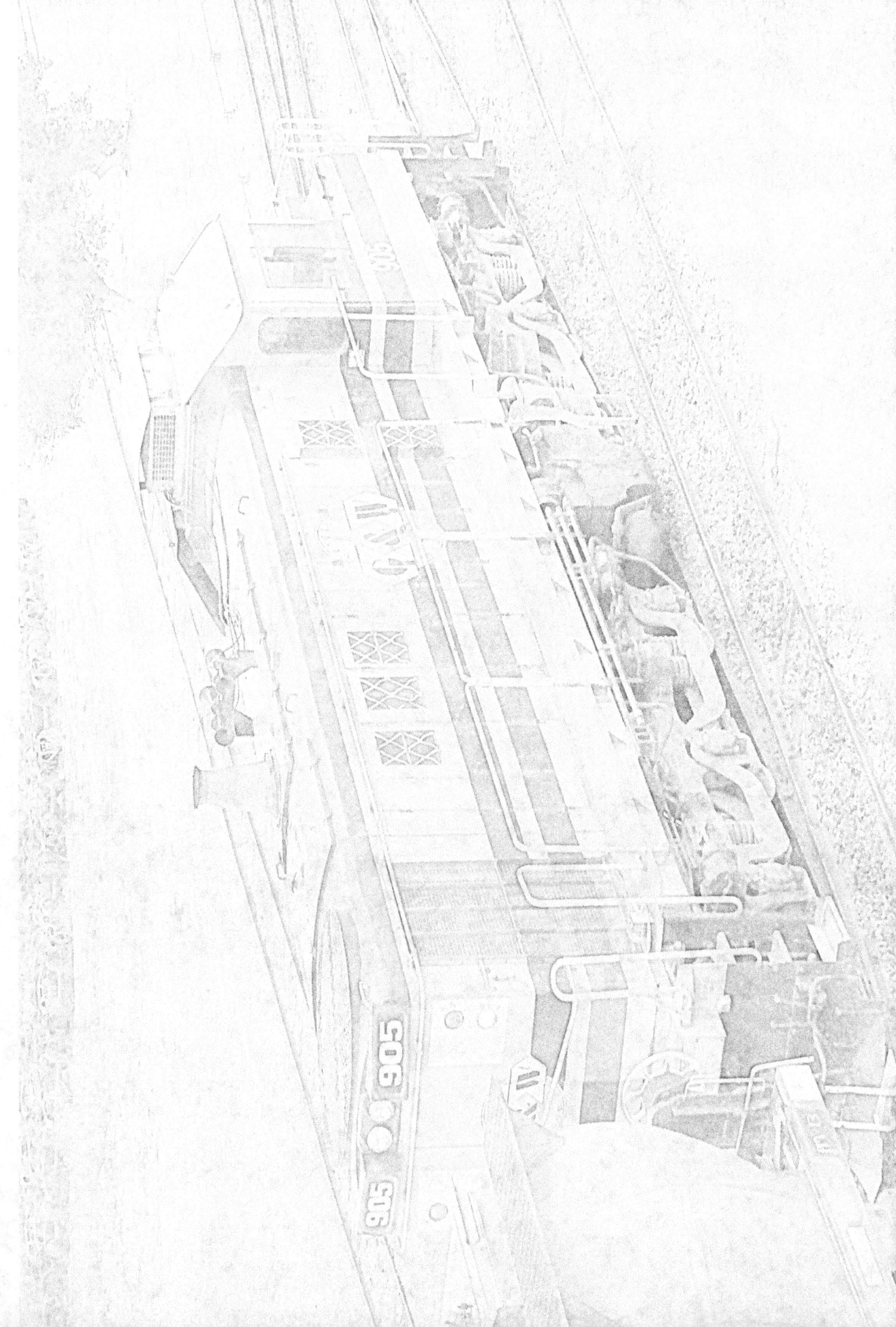

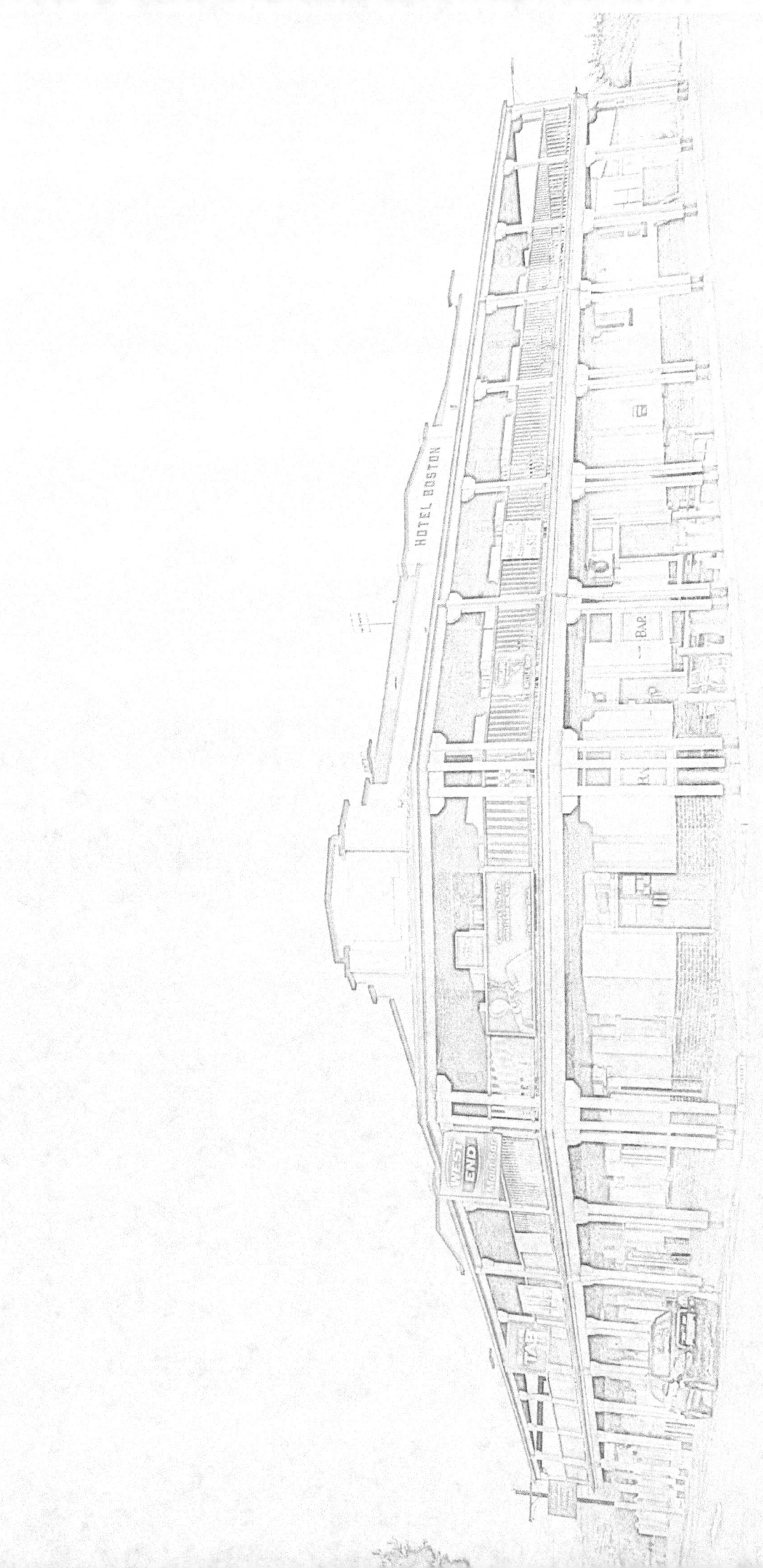

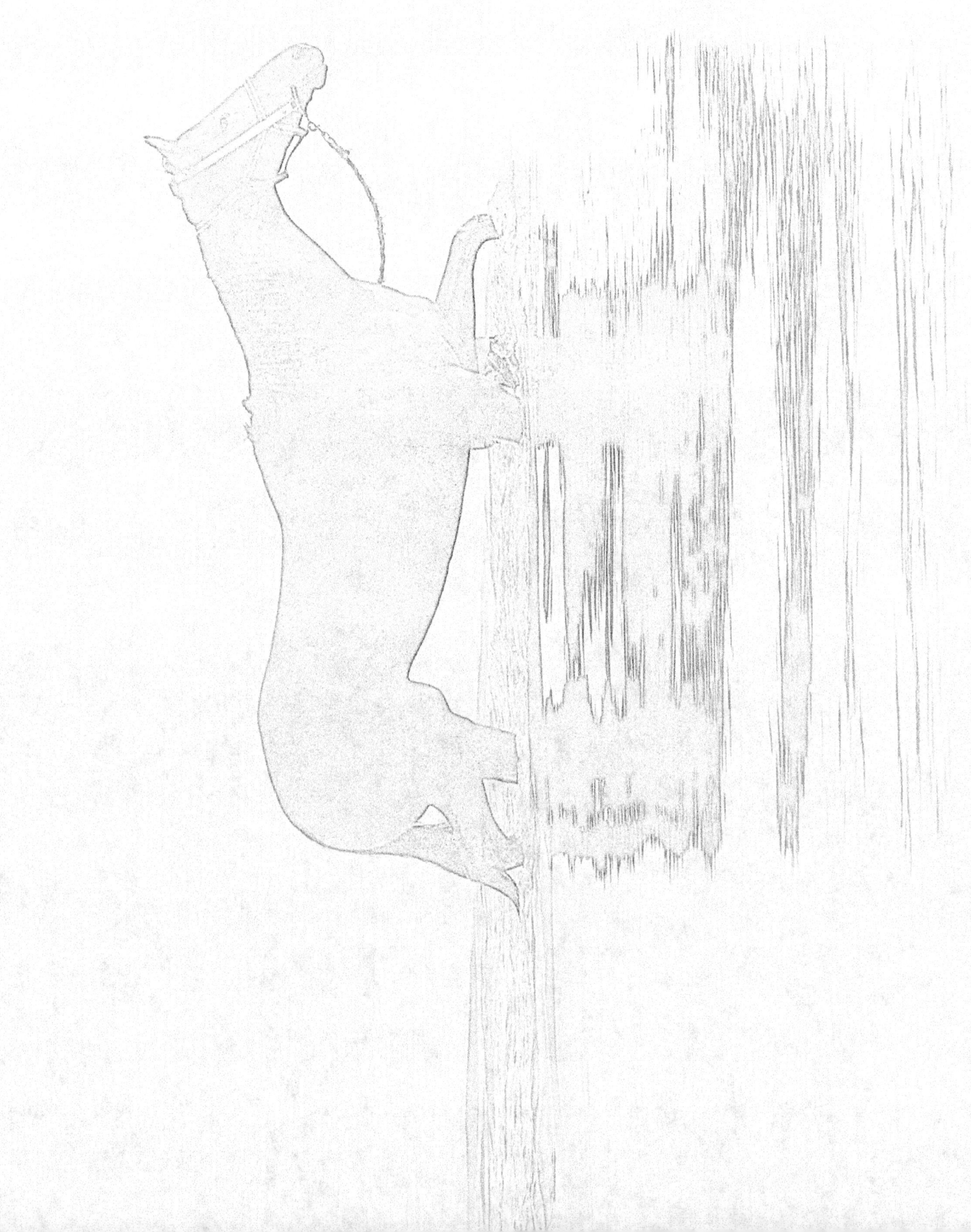

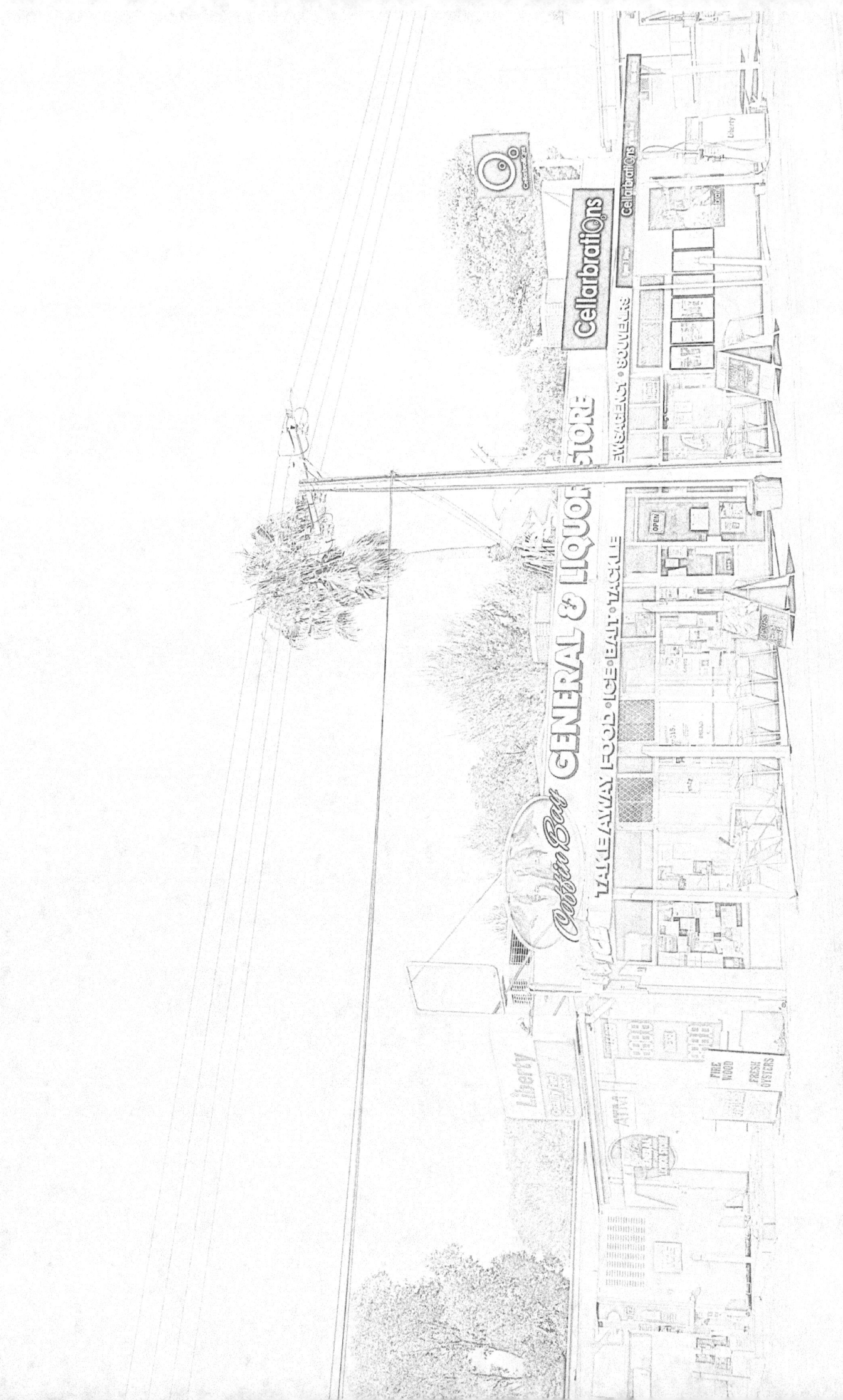

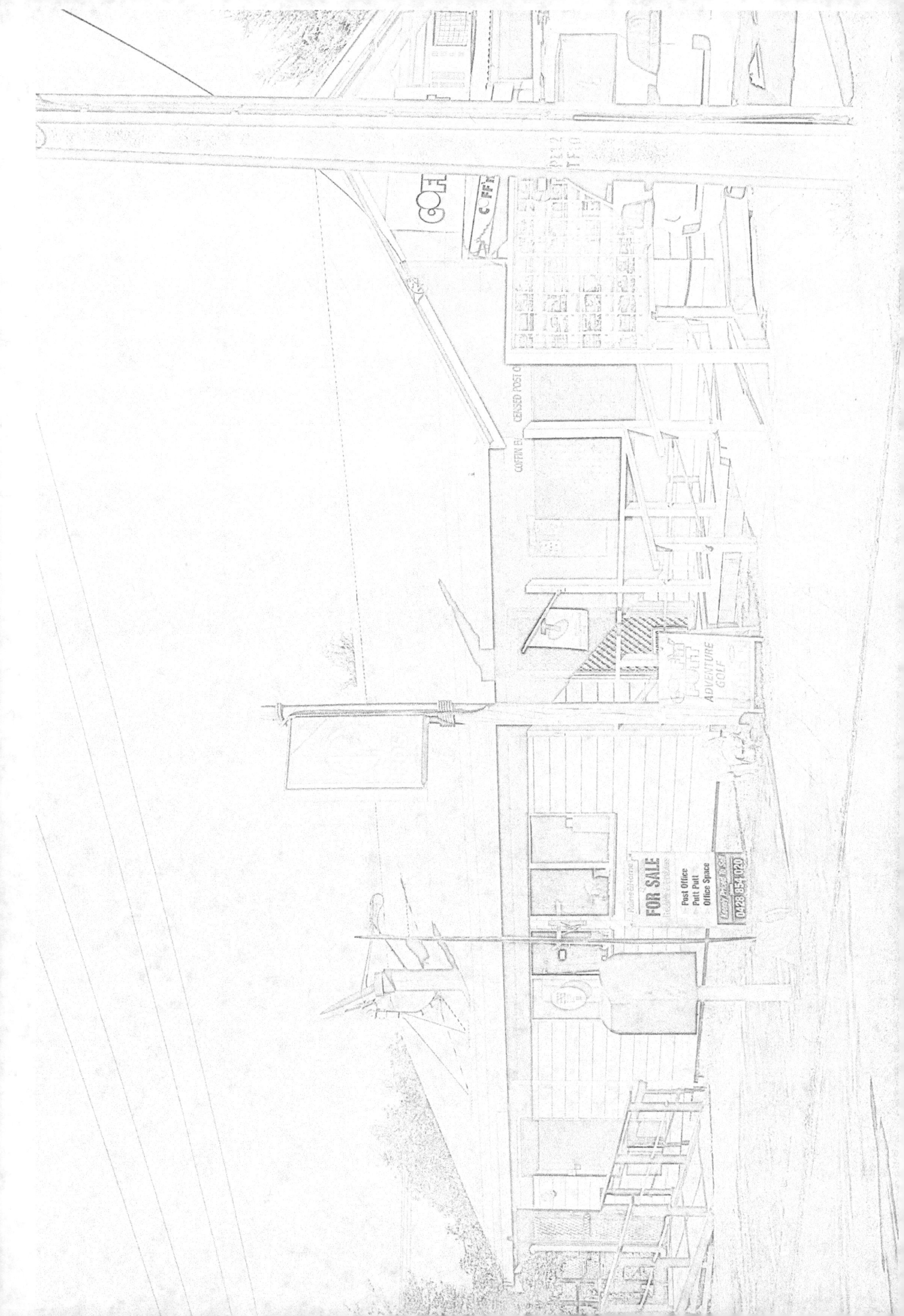

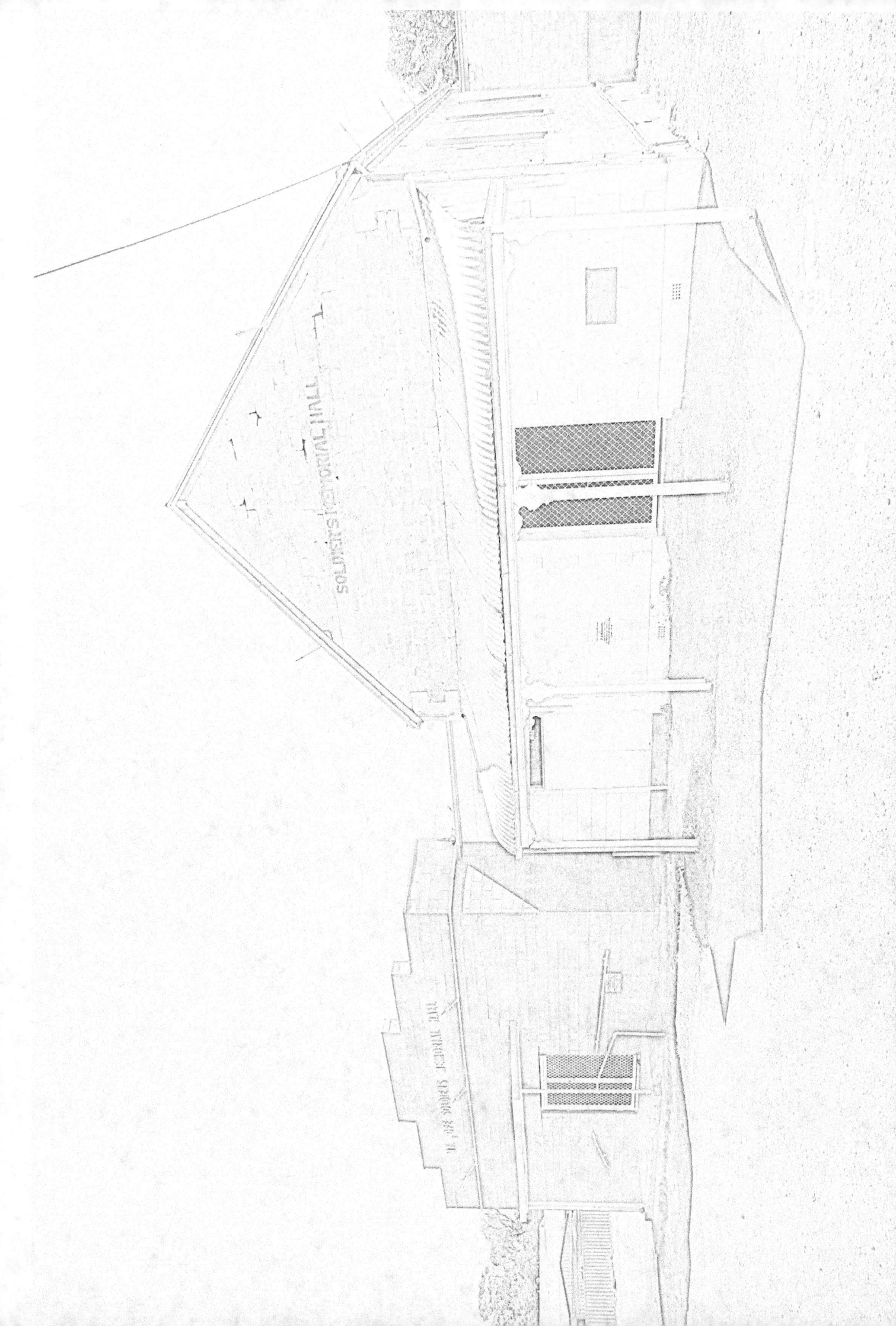

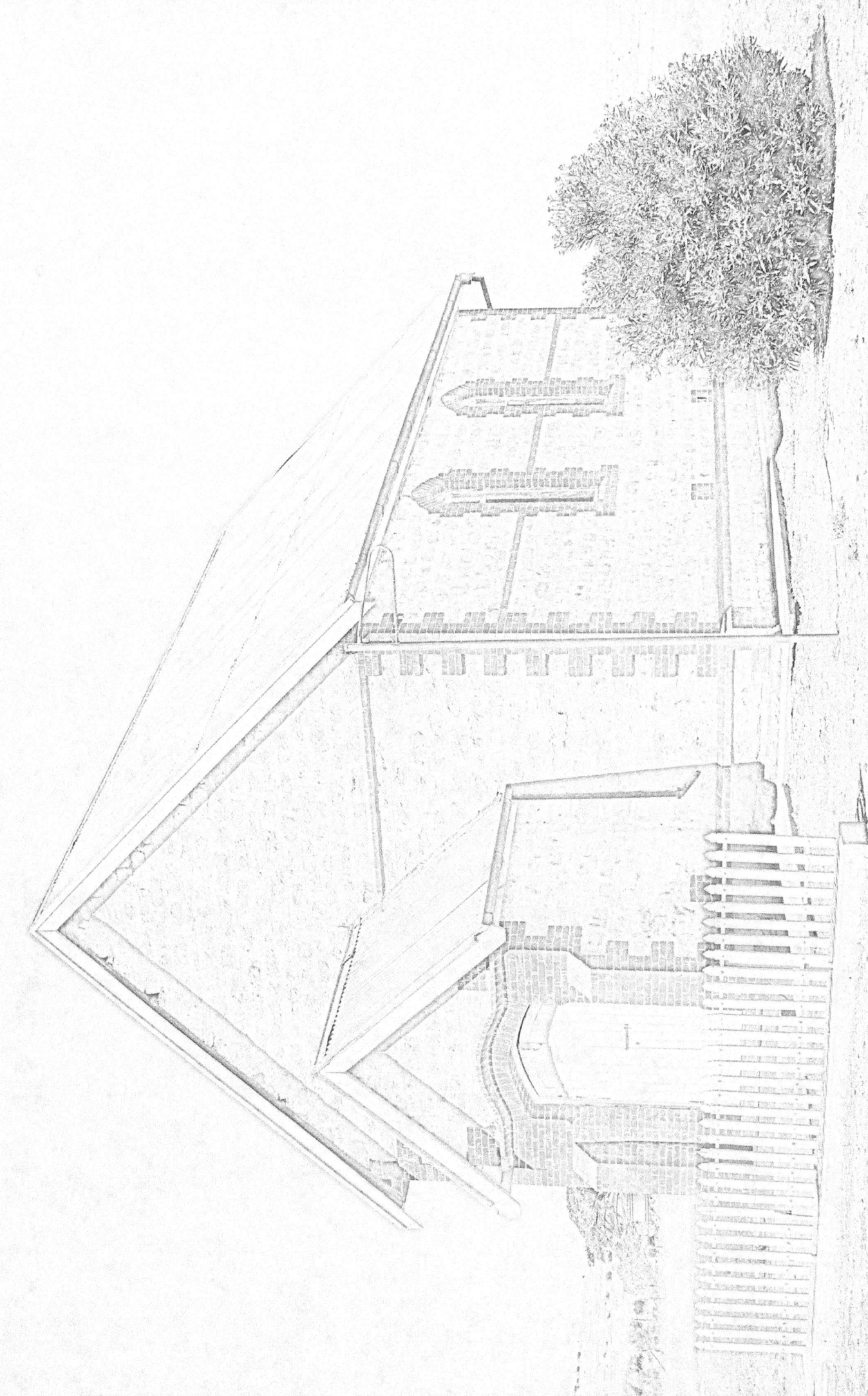

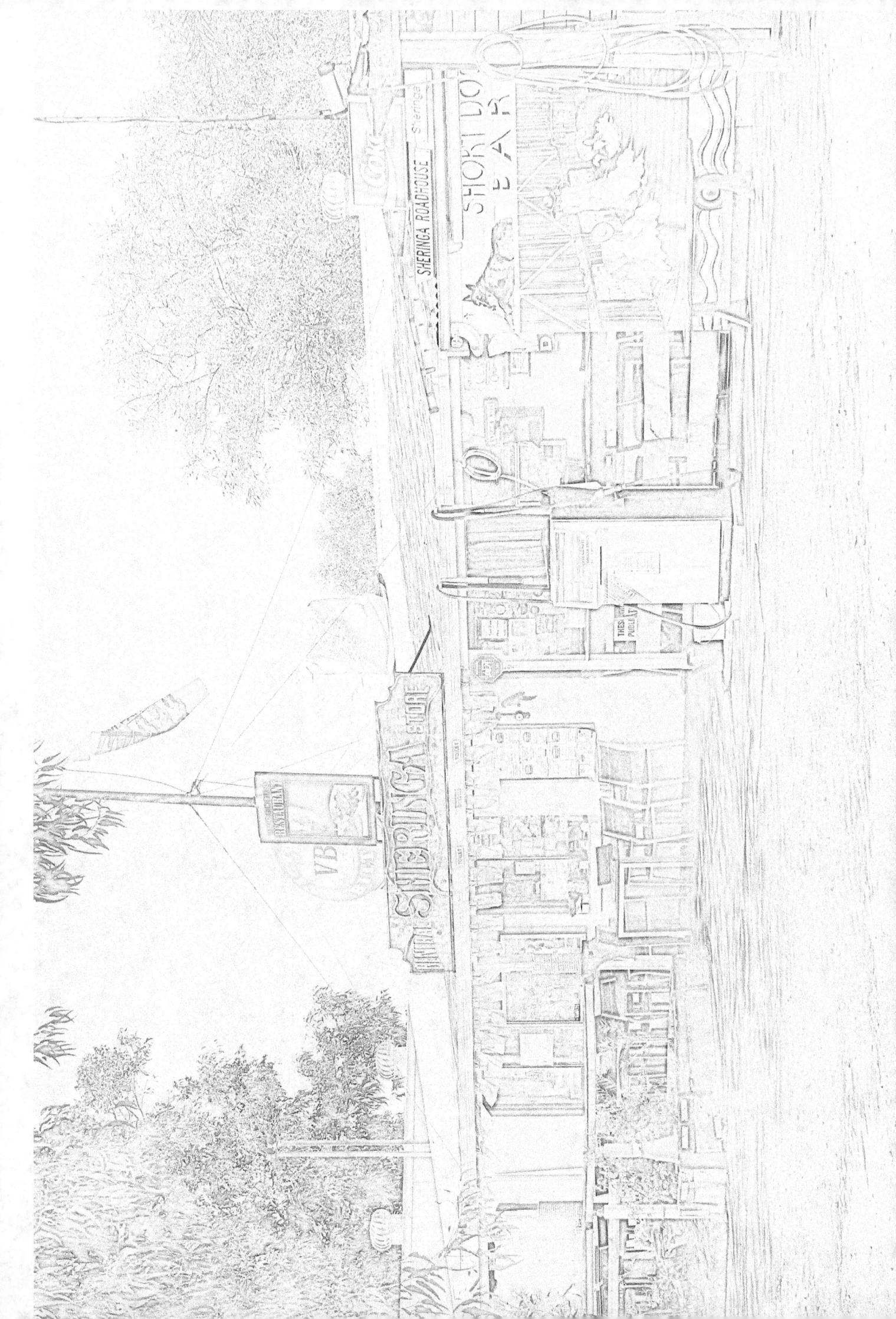

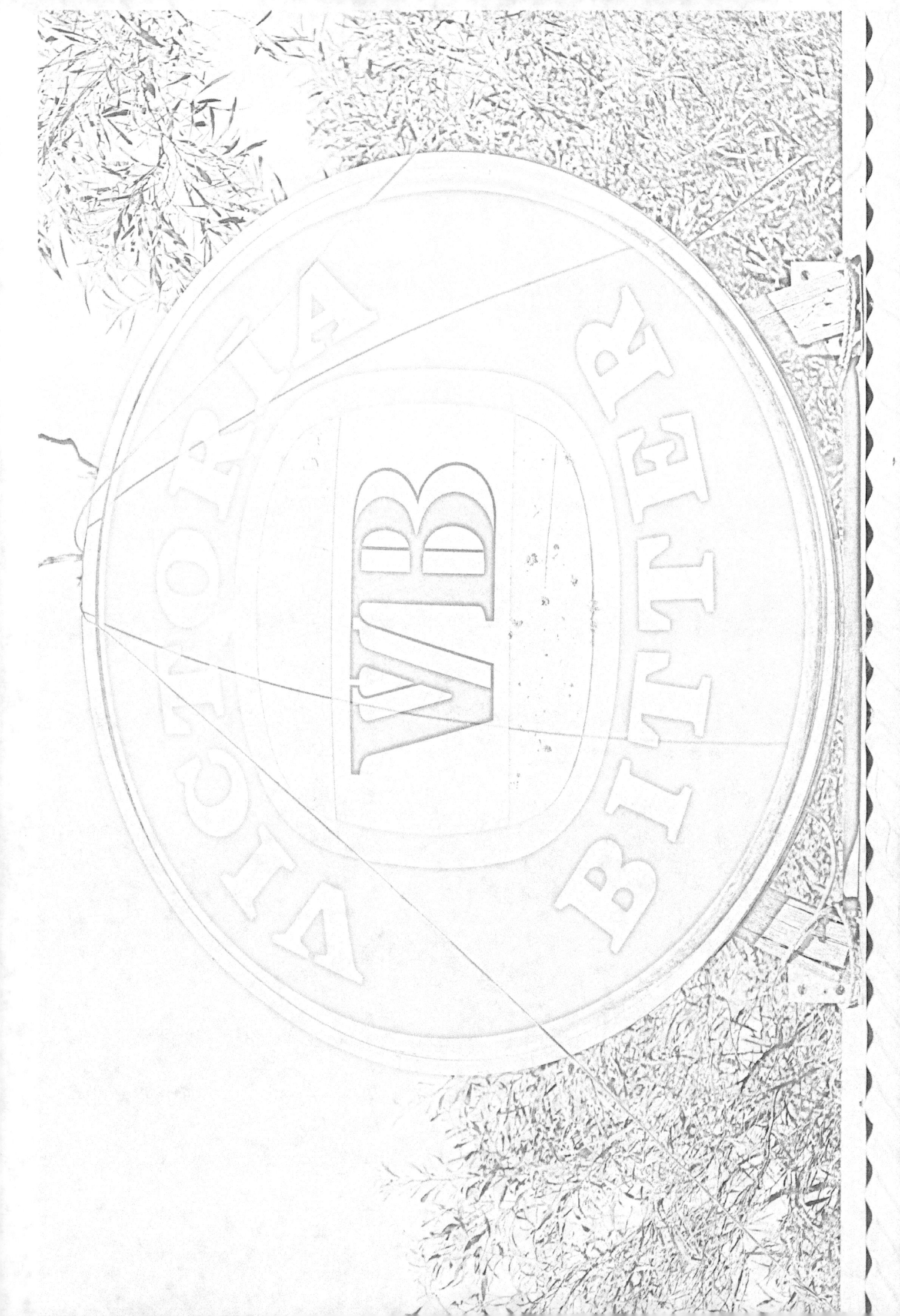

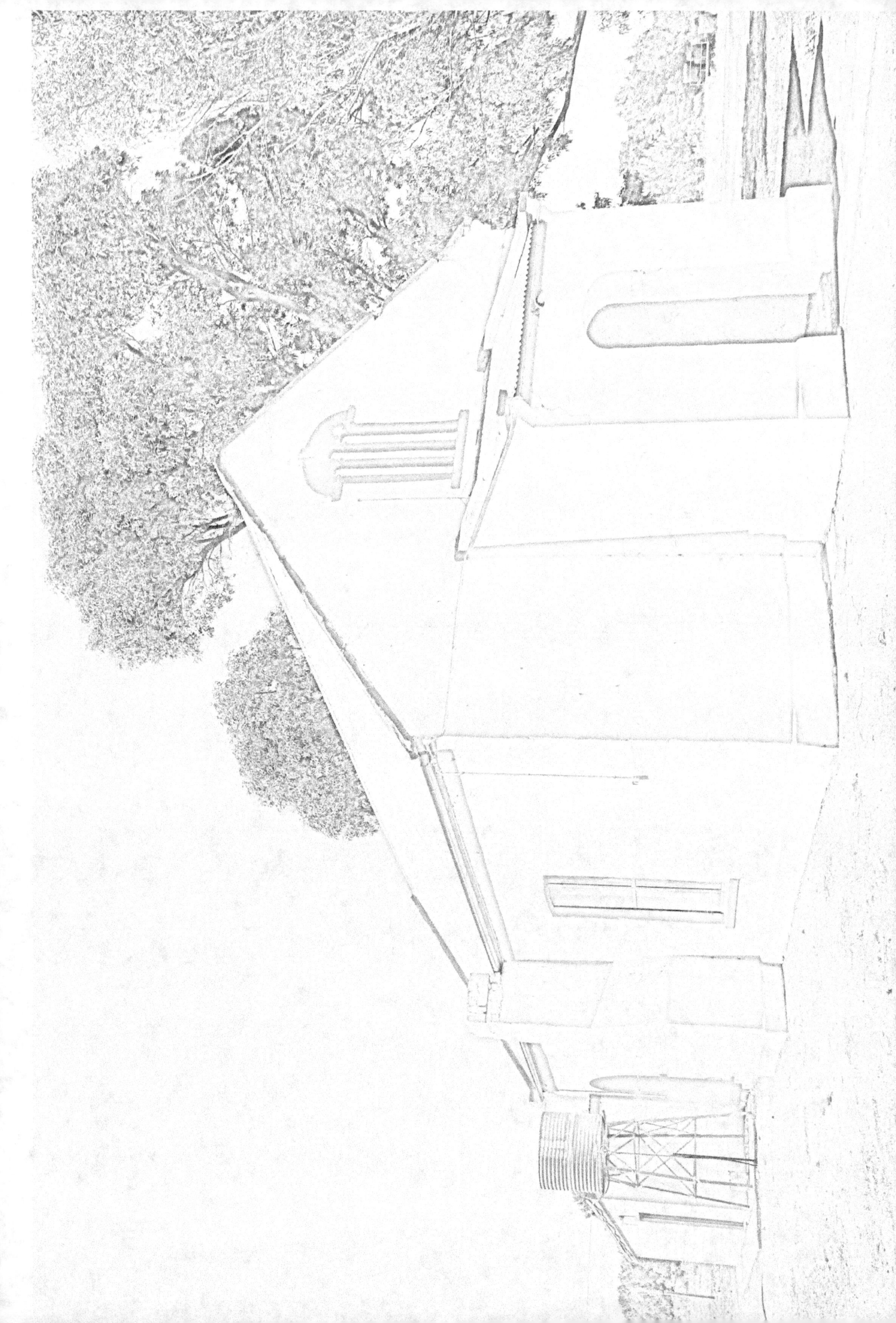

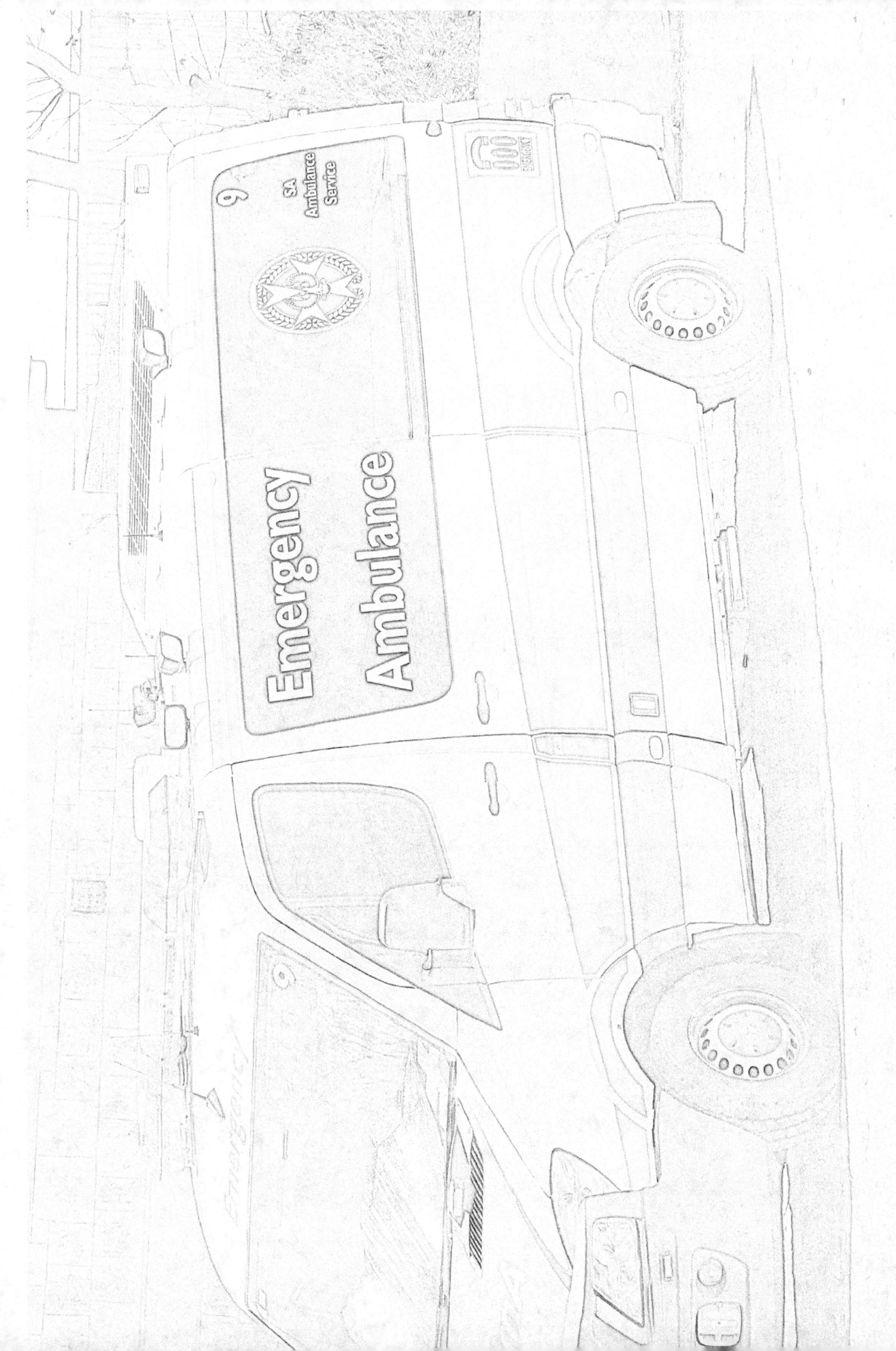

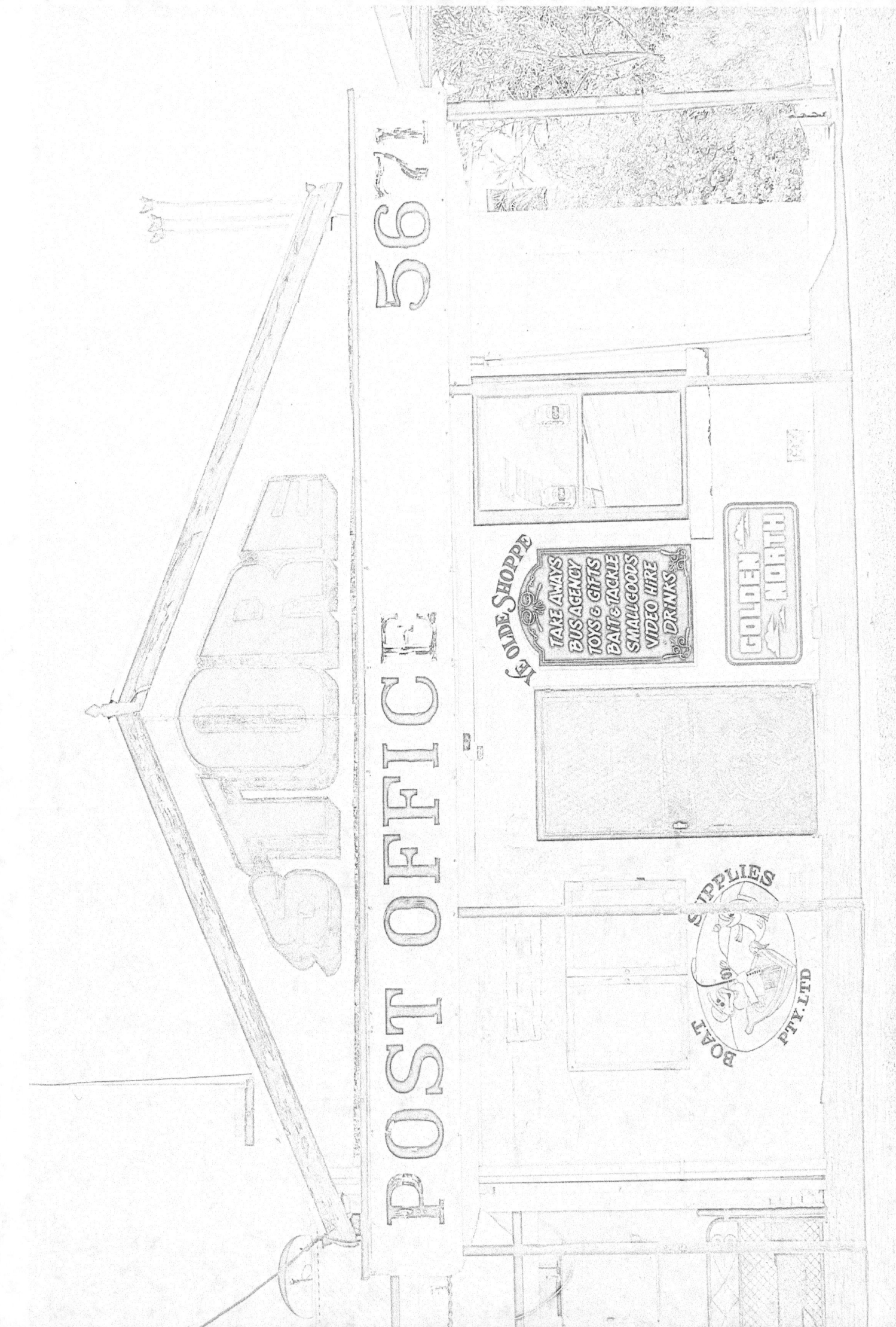

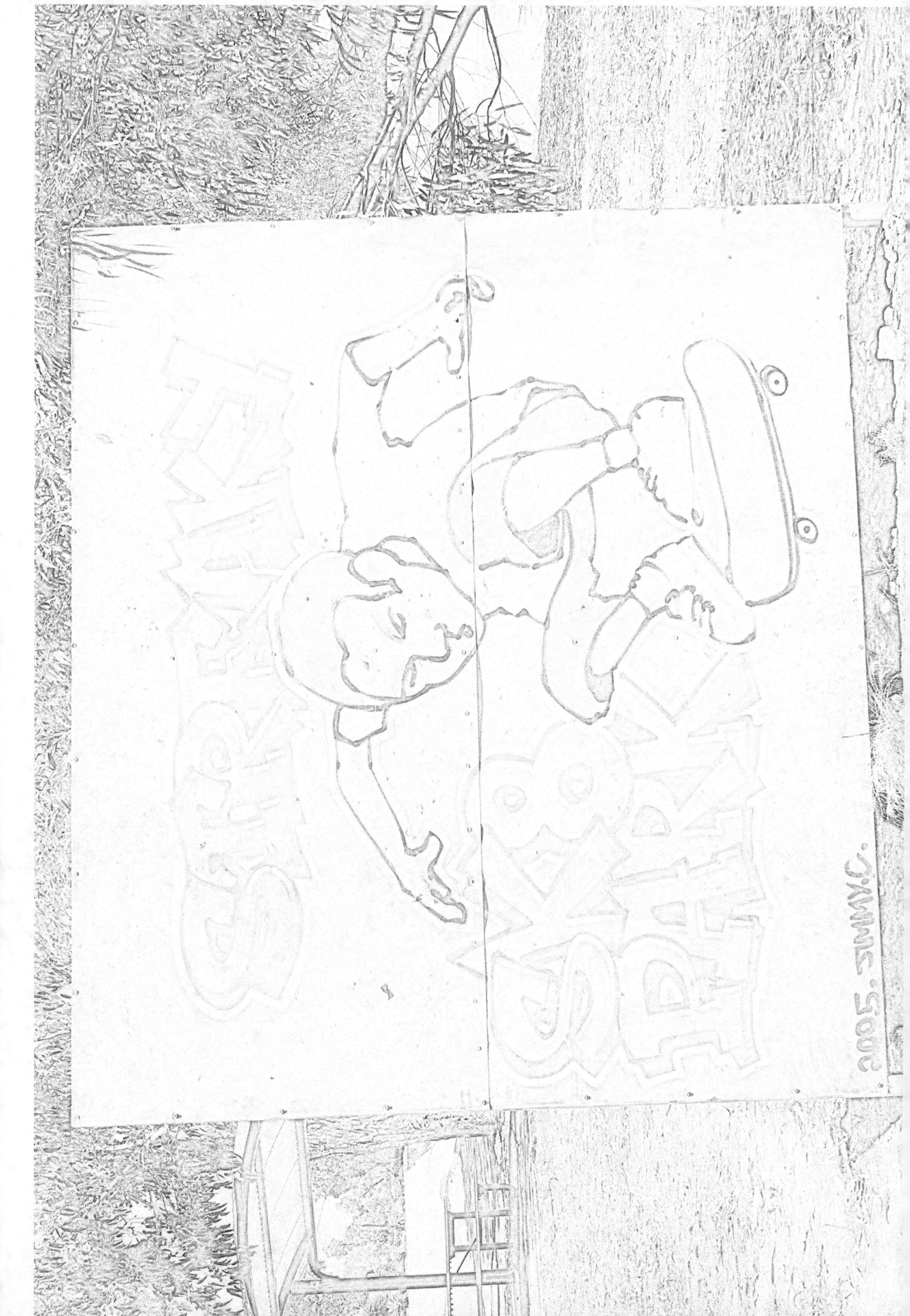

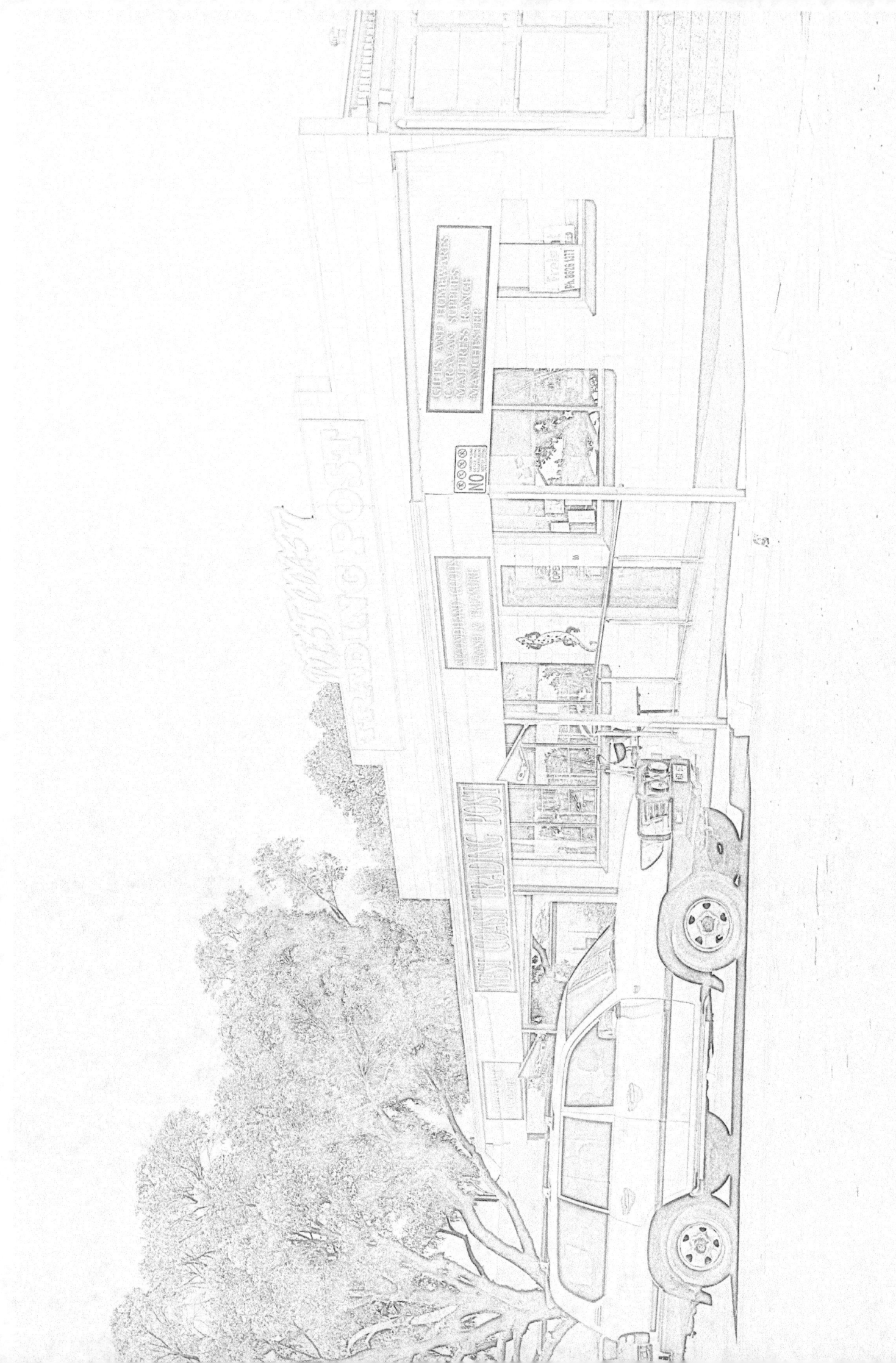

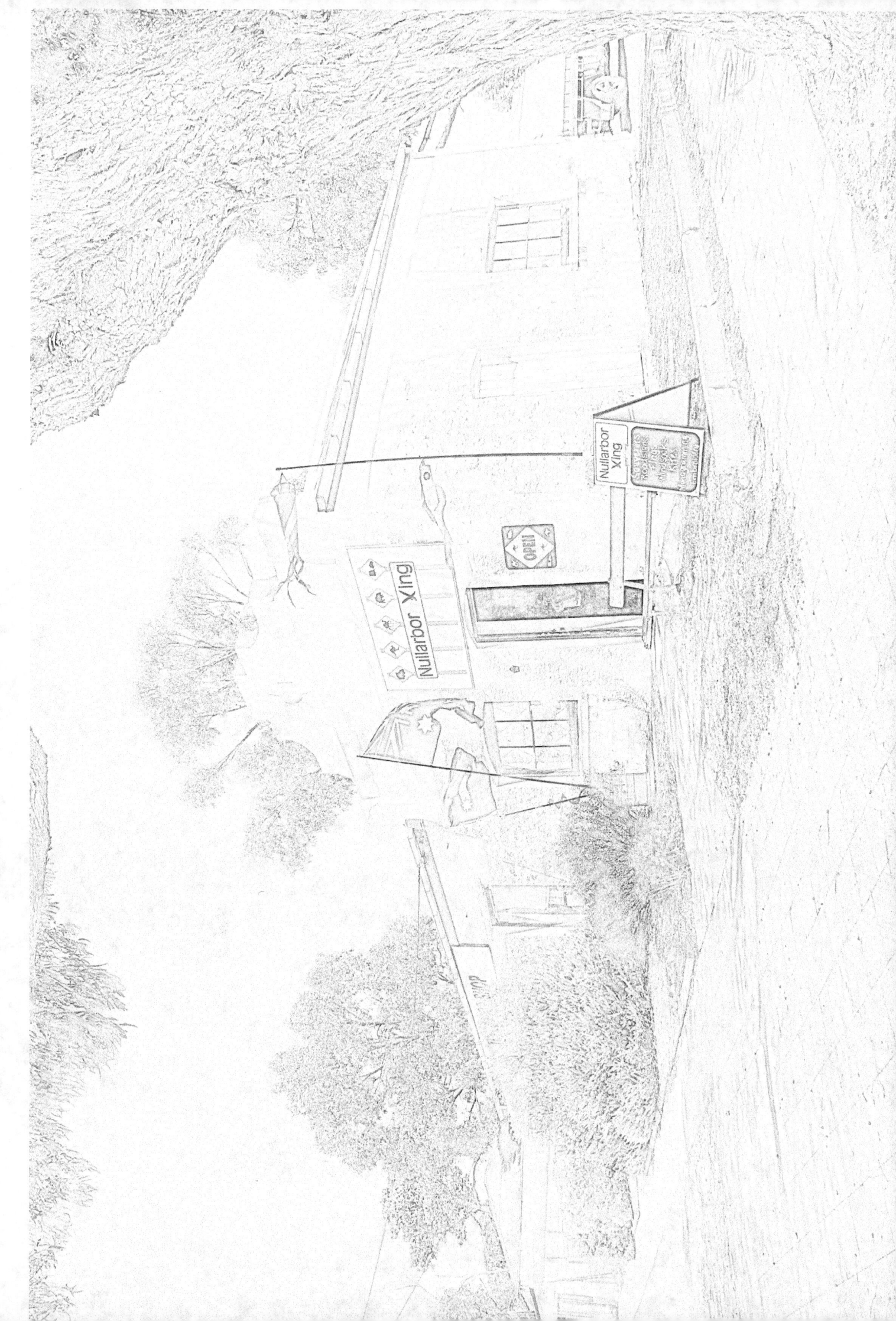

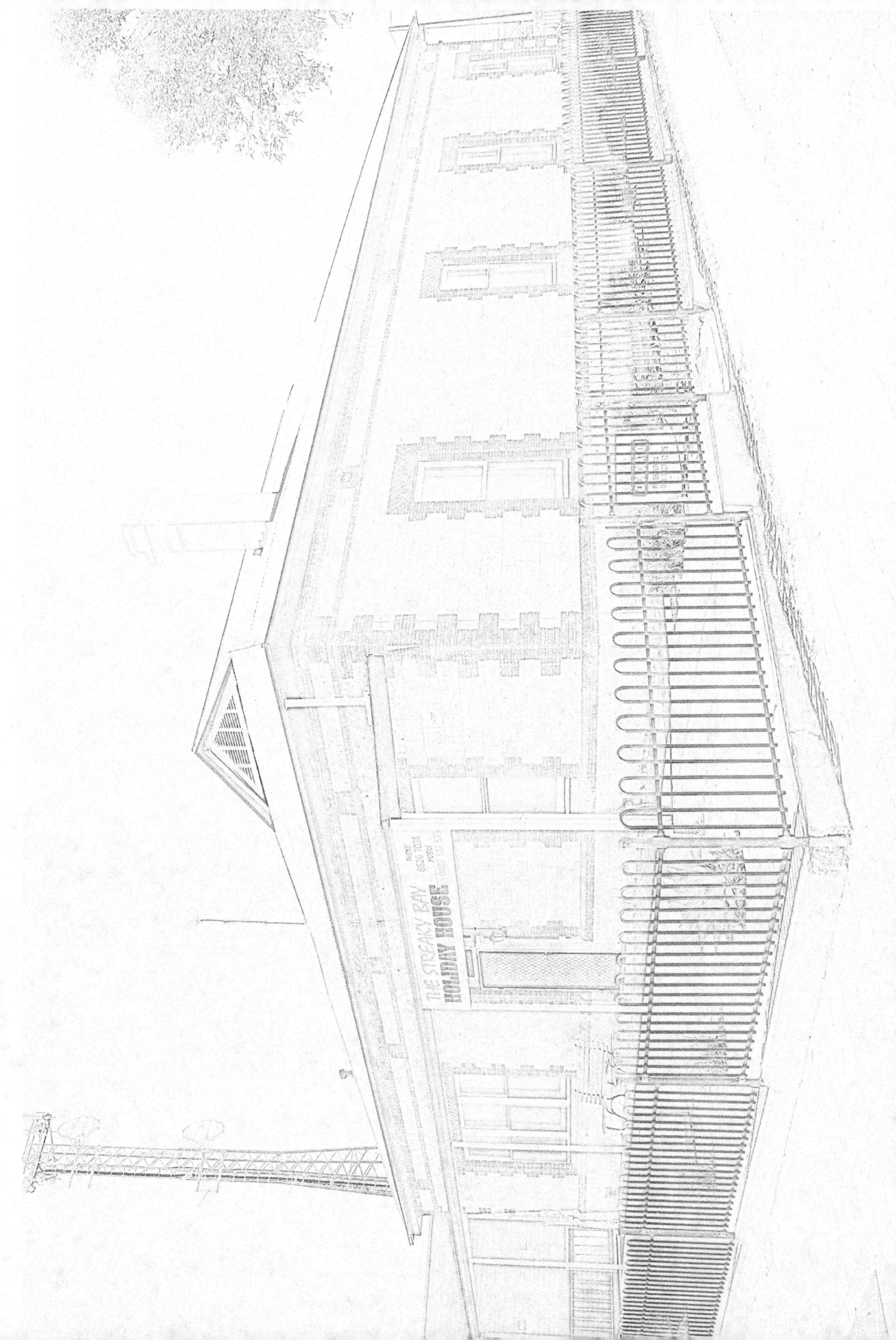

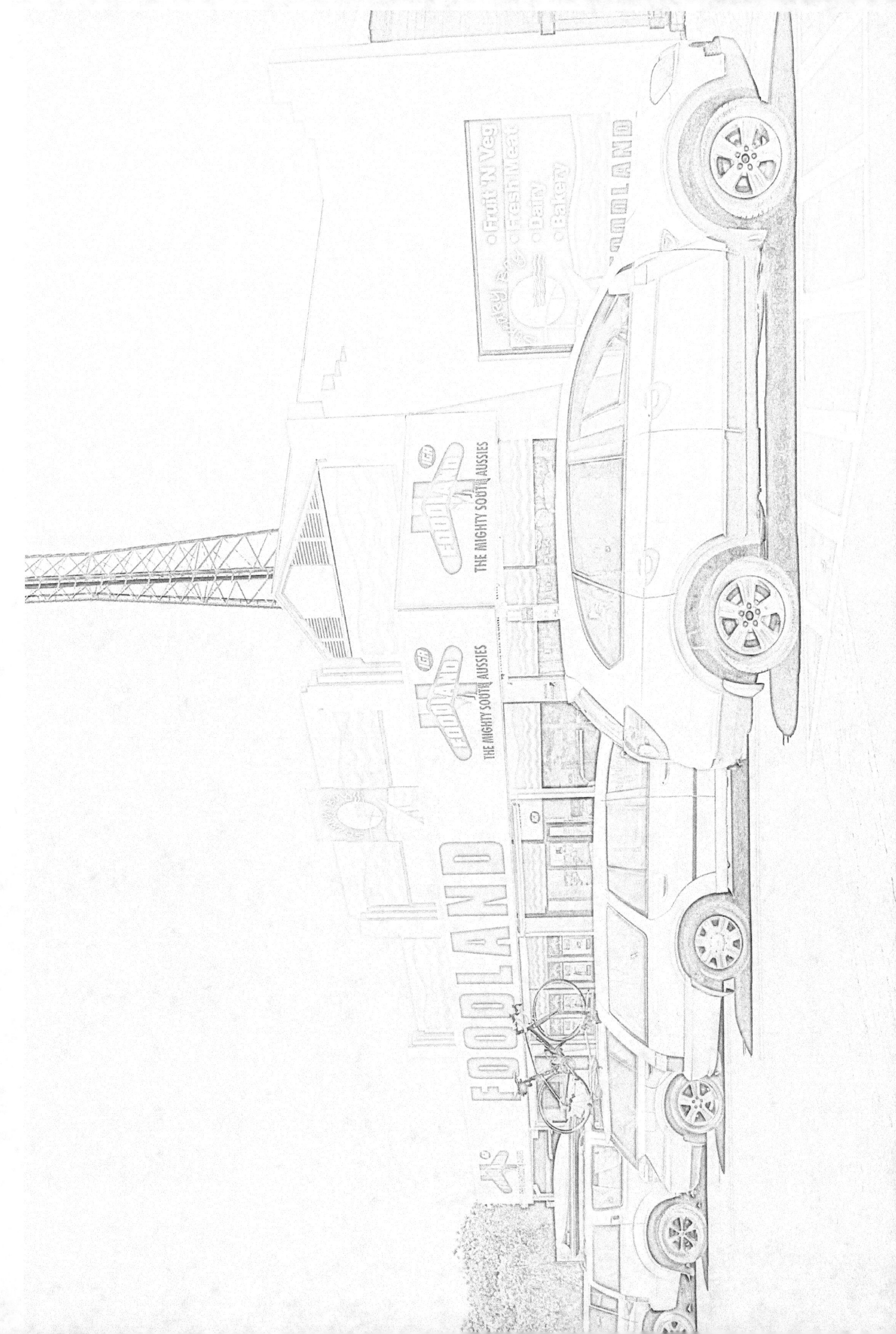

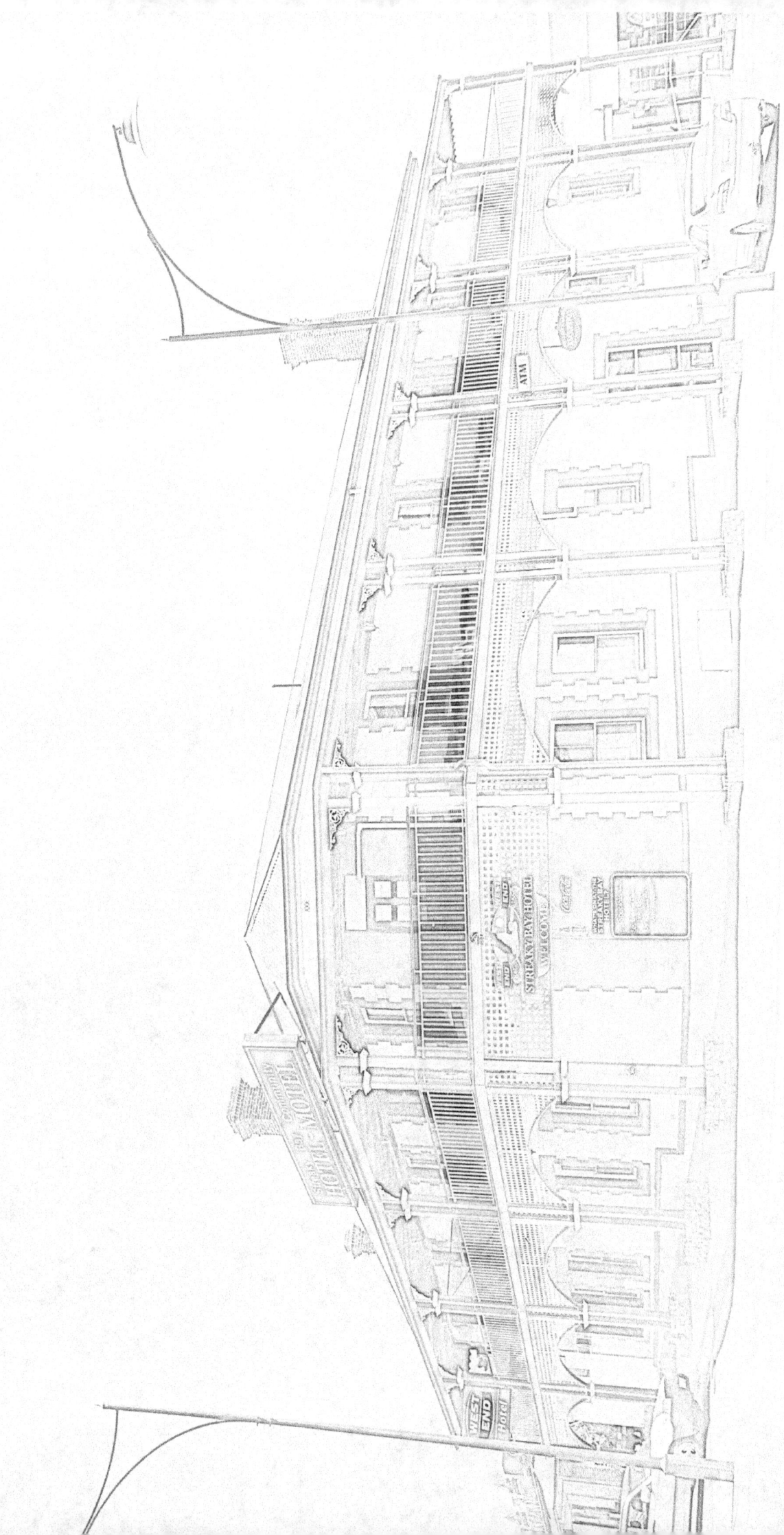

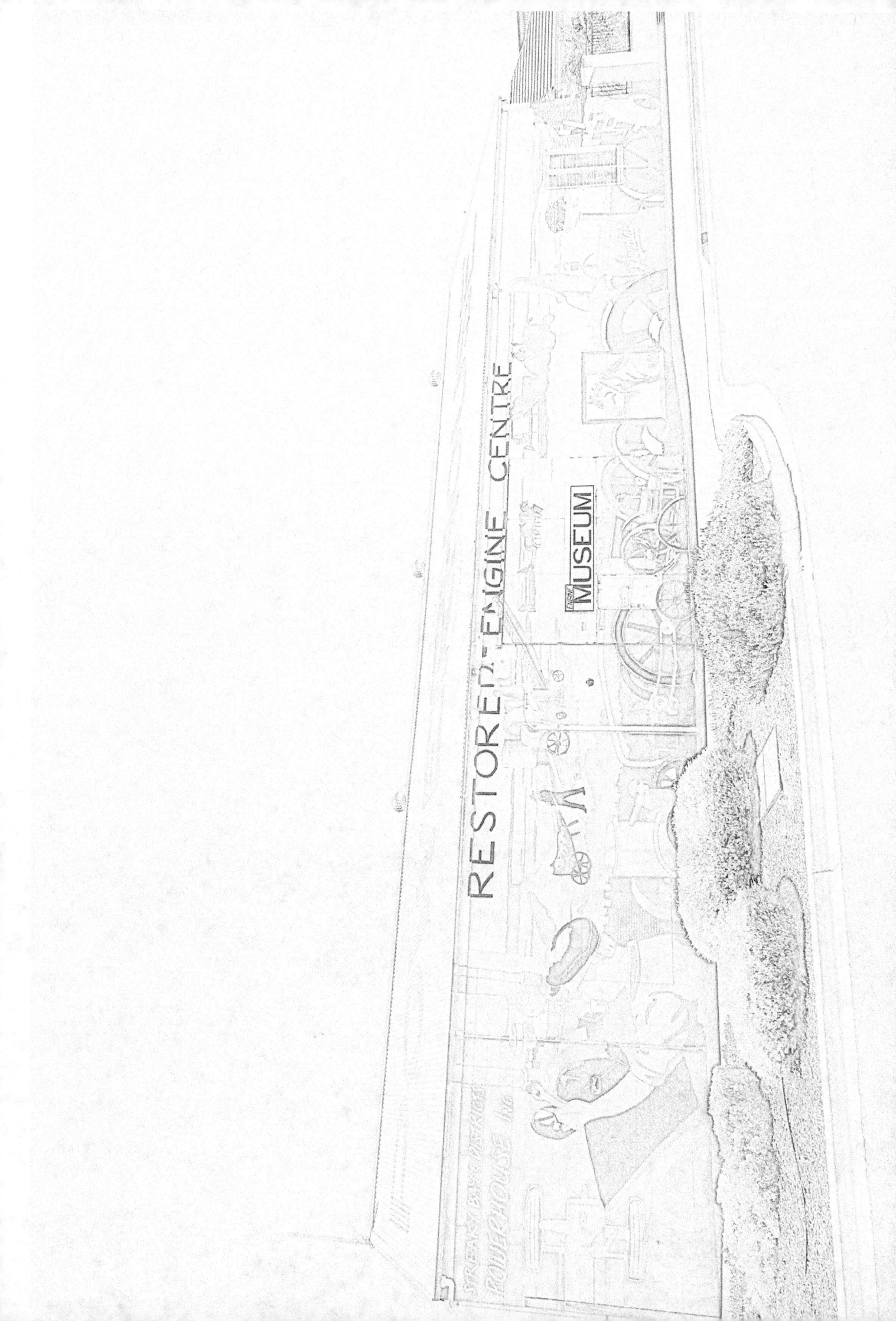

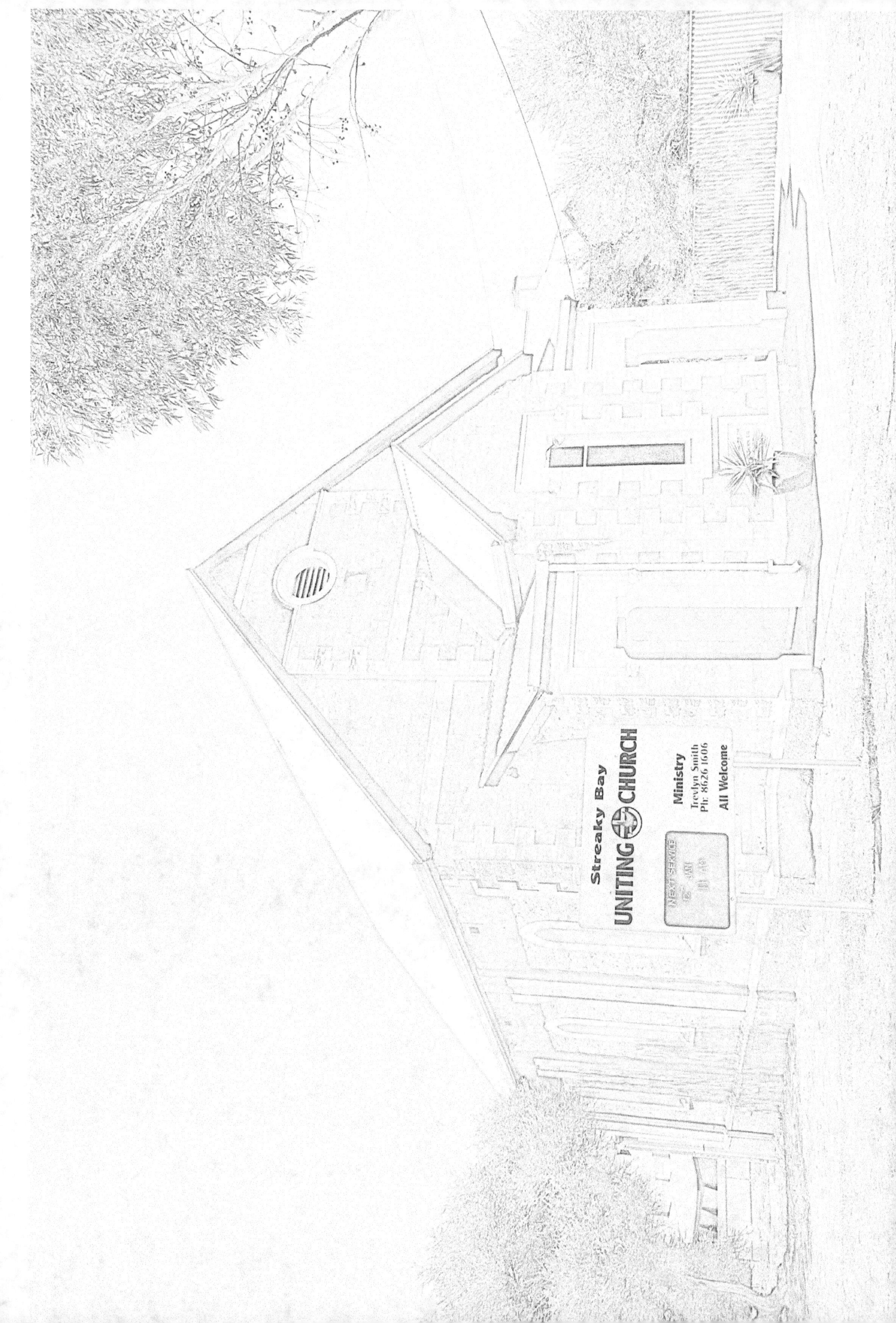

Streaky Bay
UNITING CHURCH

NEXT SERVICE

Ministry
Trevlyn Smith
Ph: 8626 1606

All Welcome

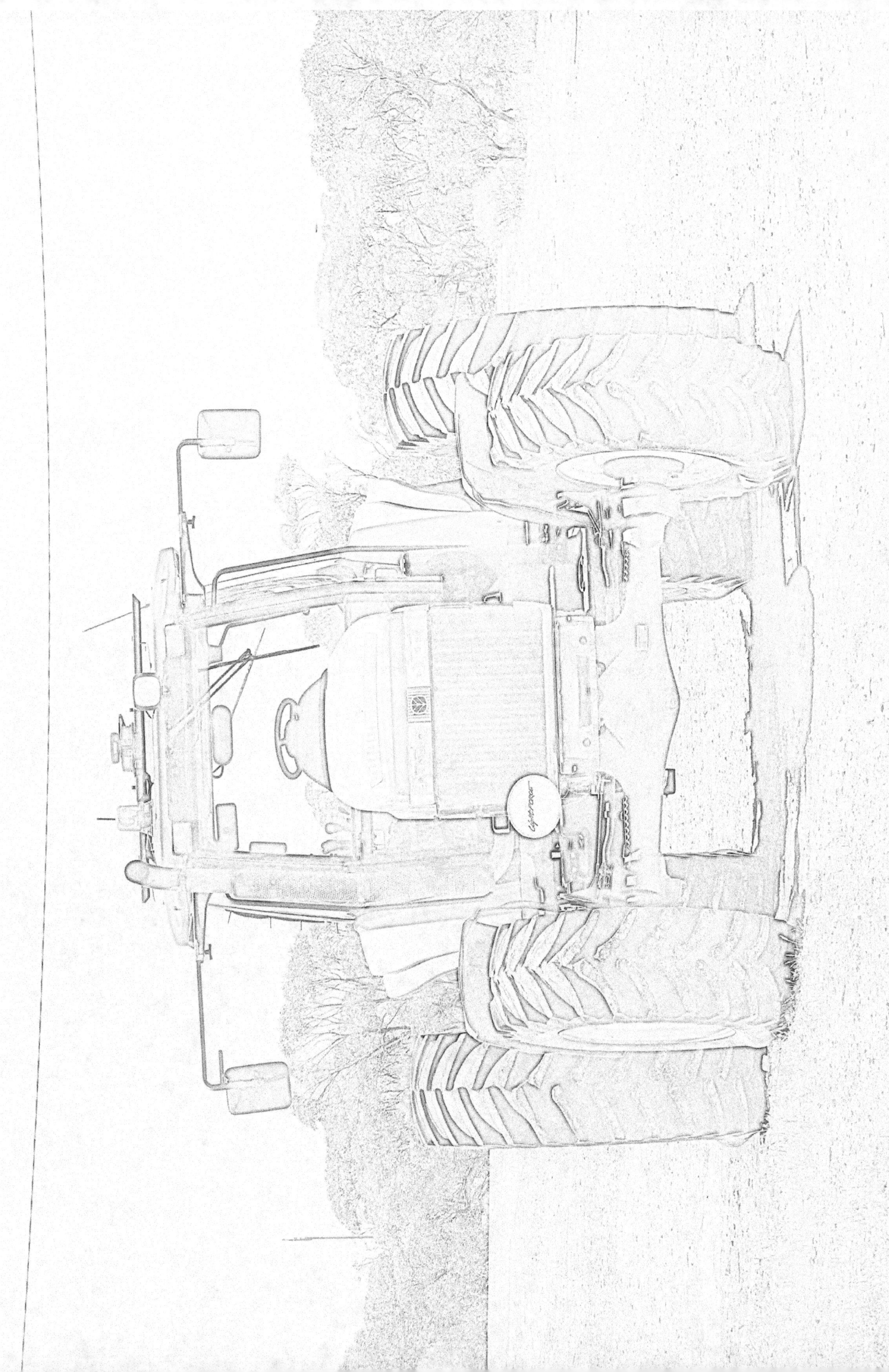

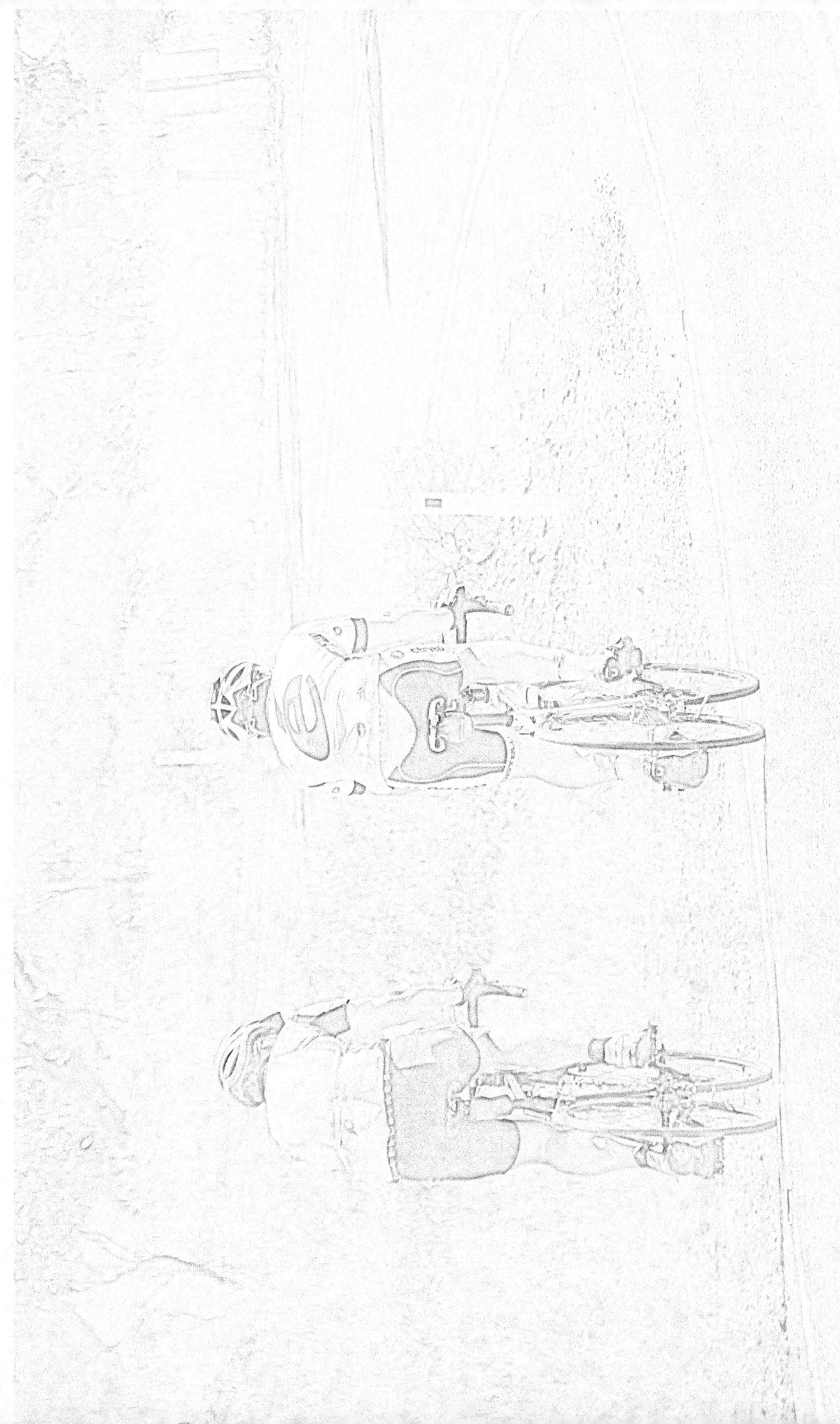

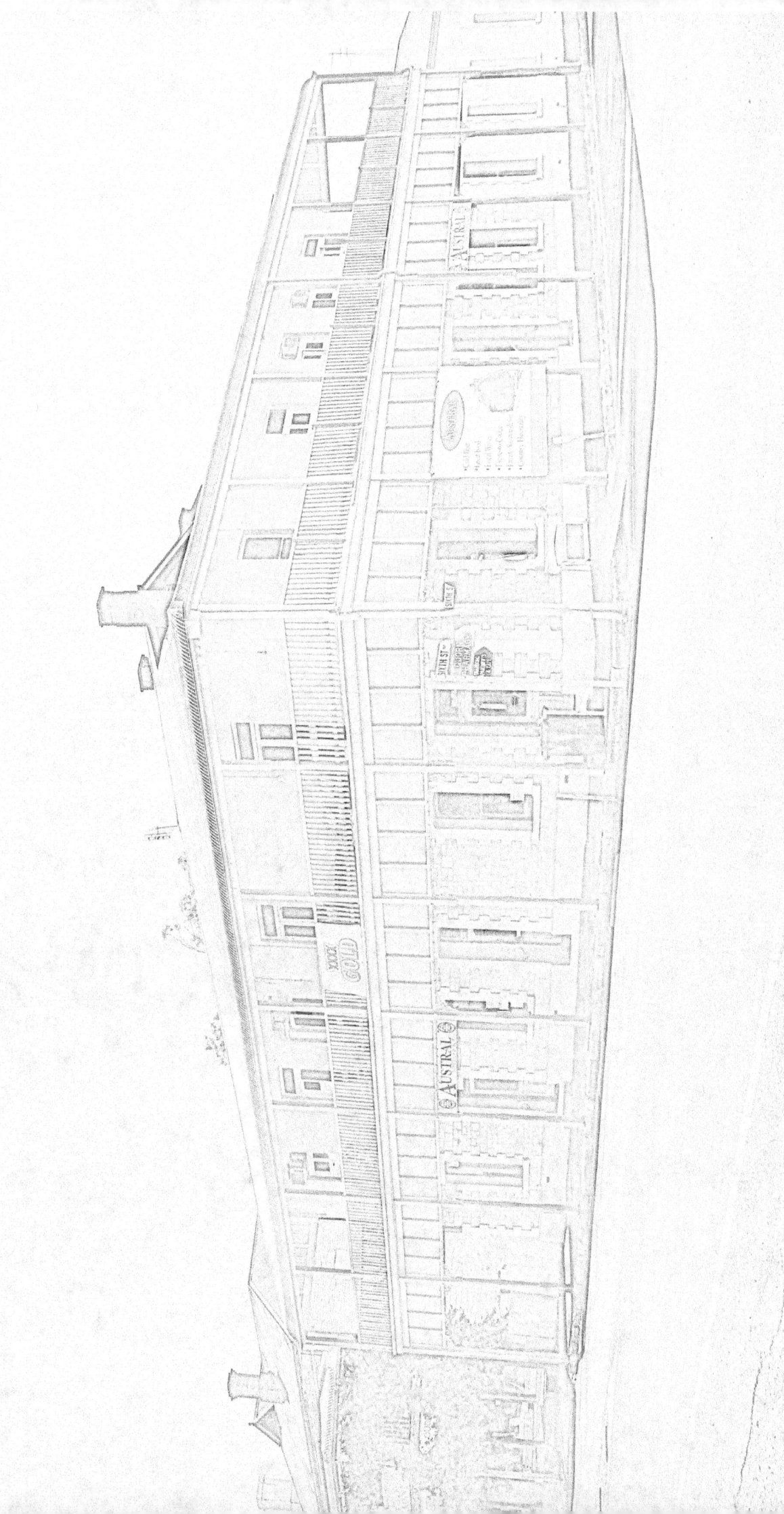

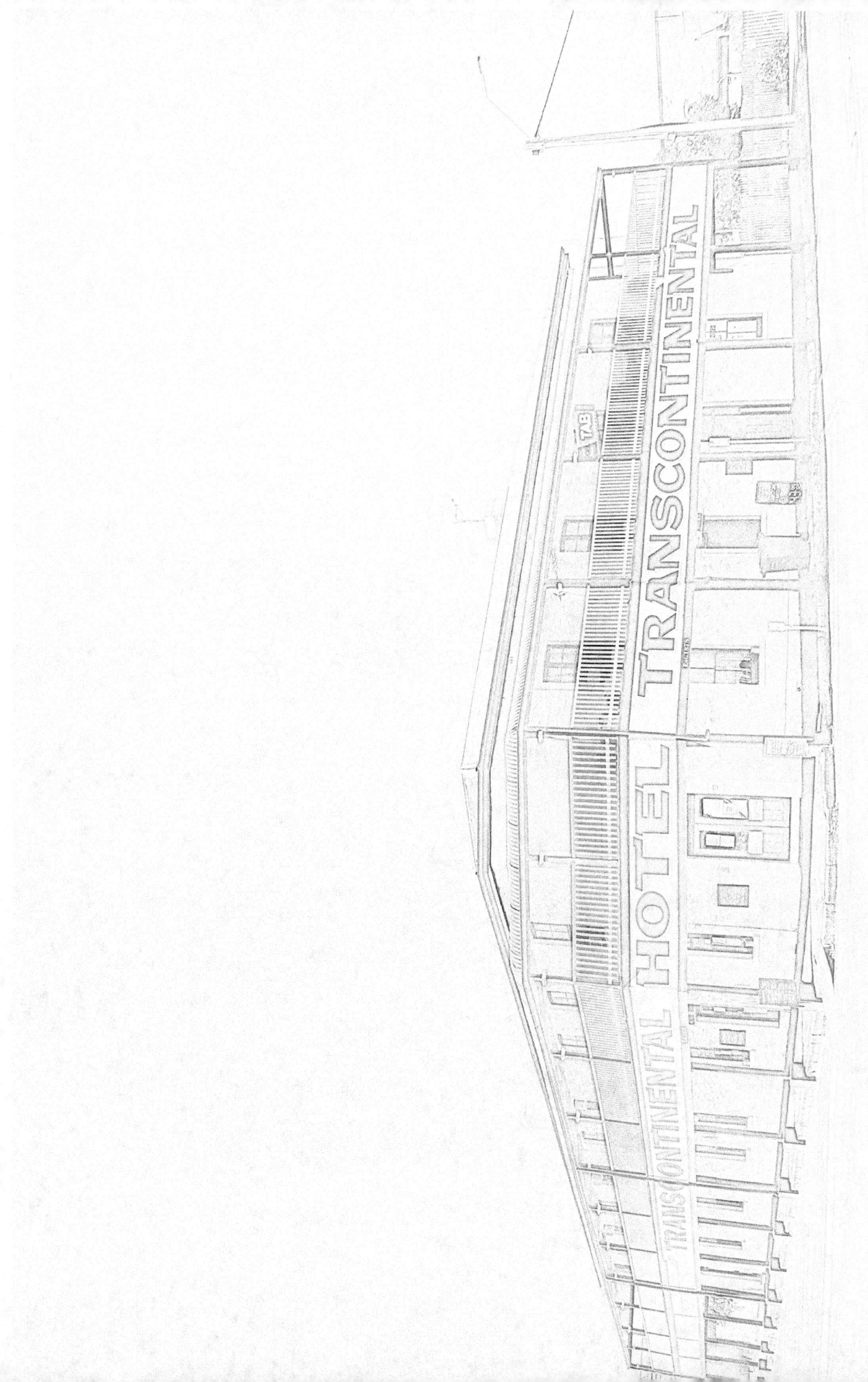

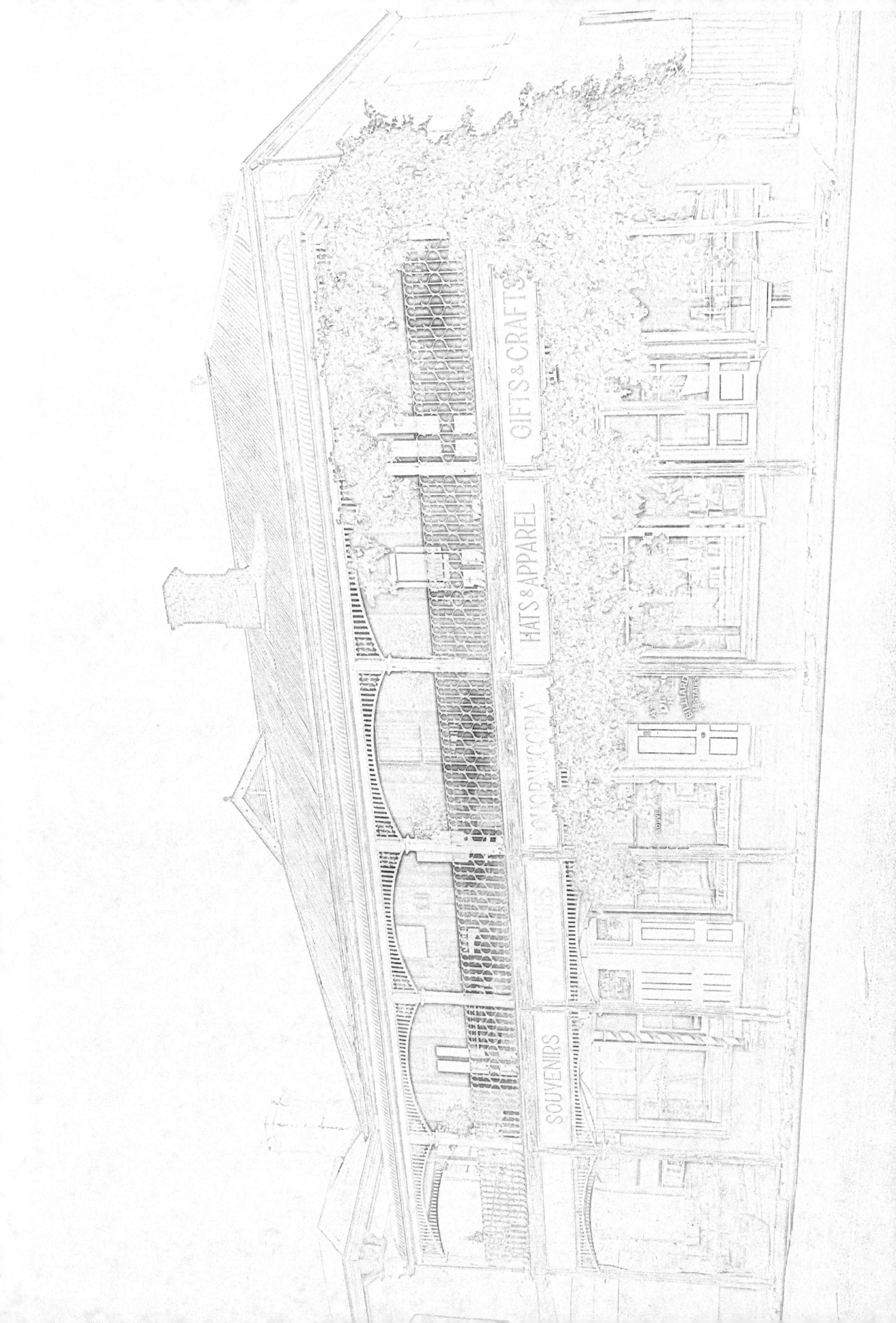

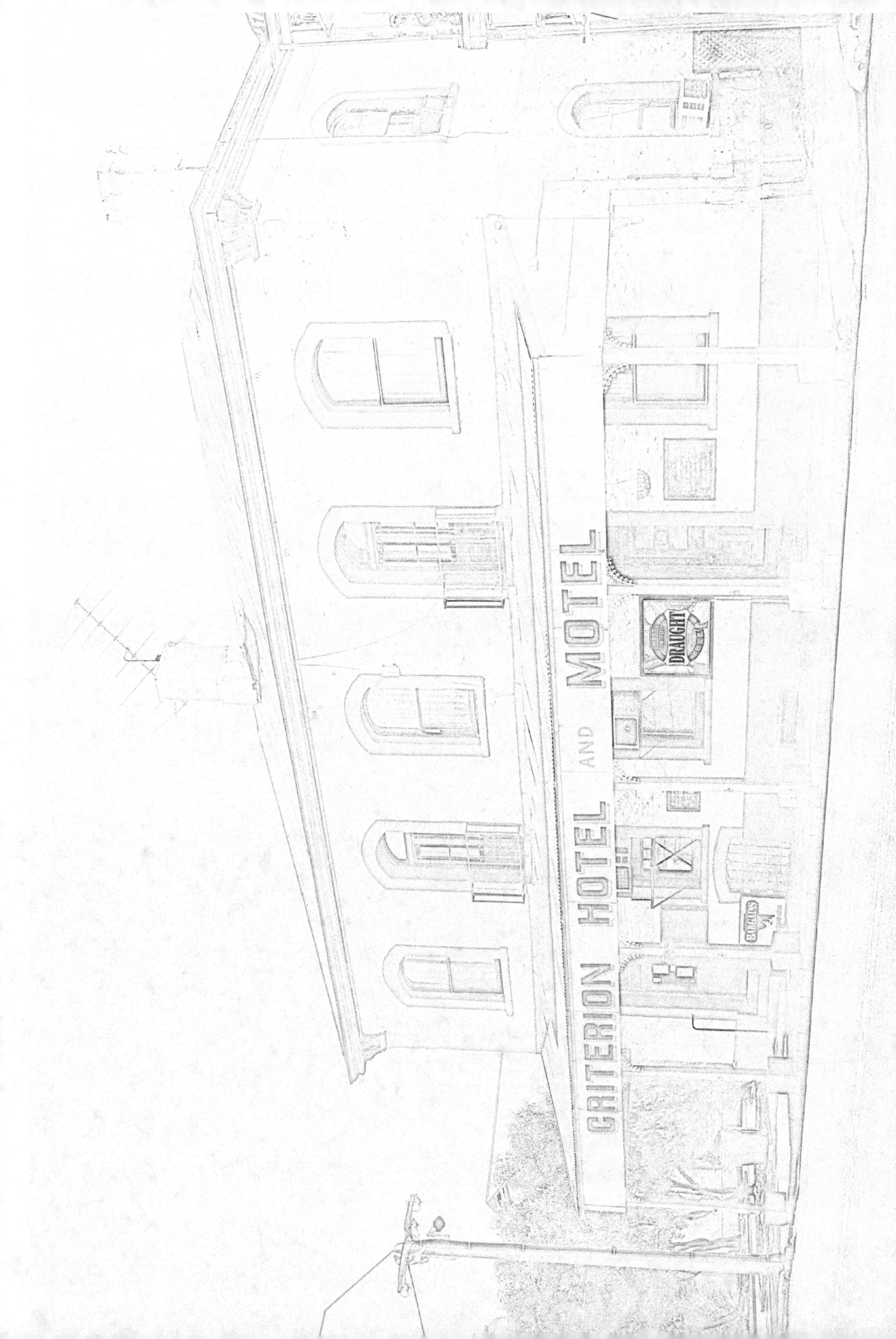

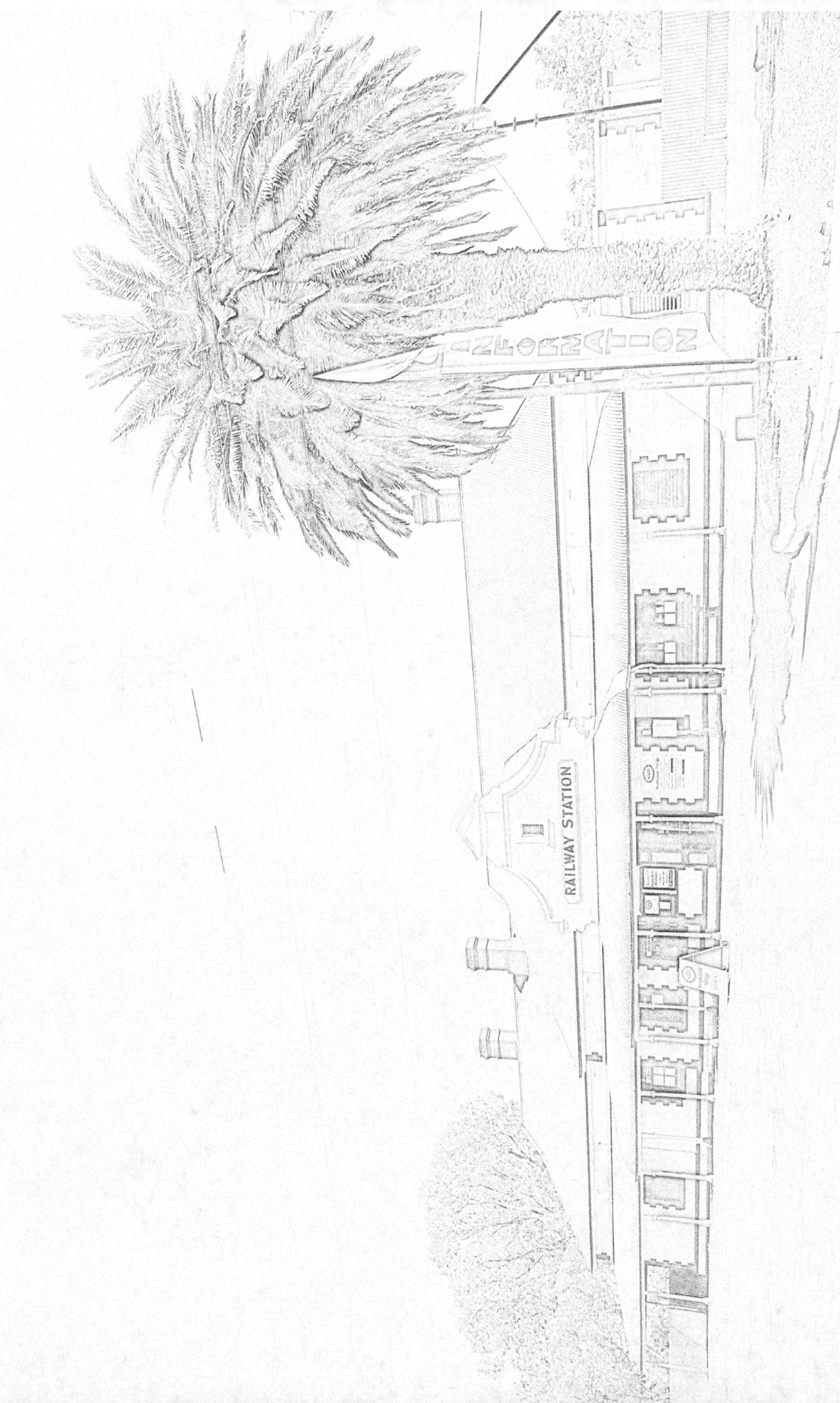

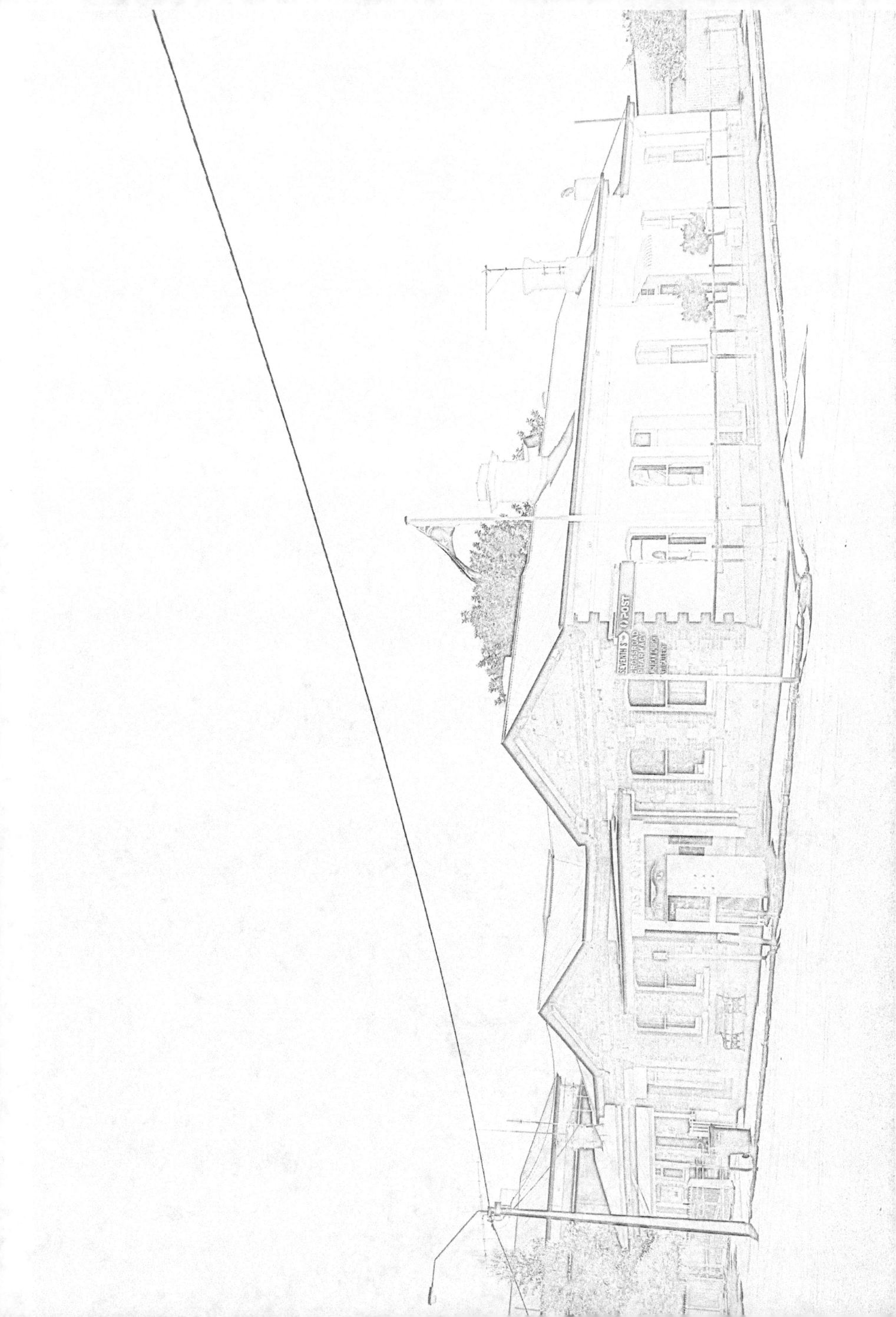

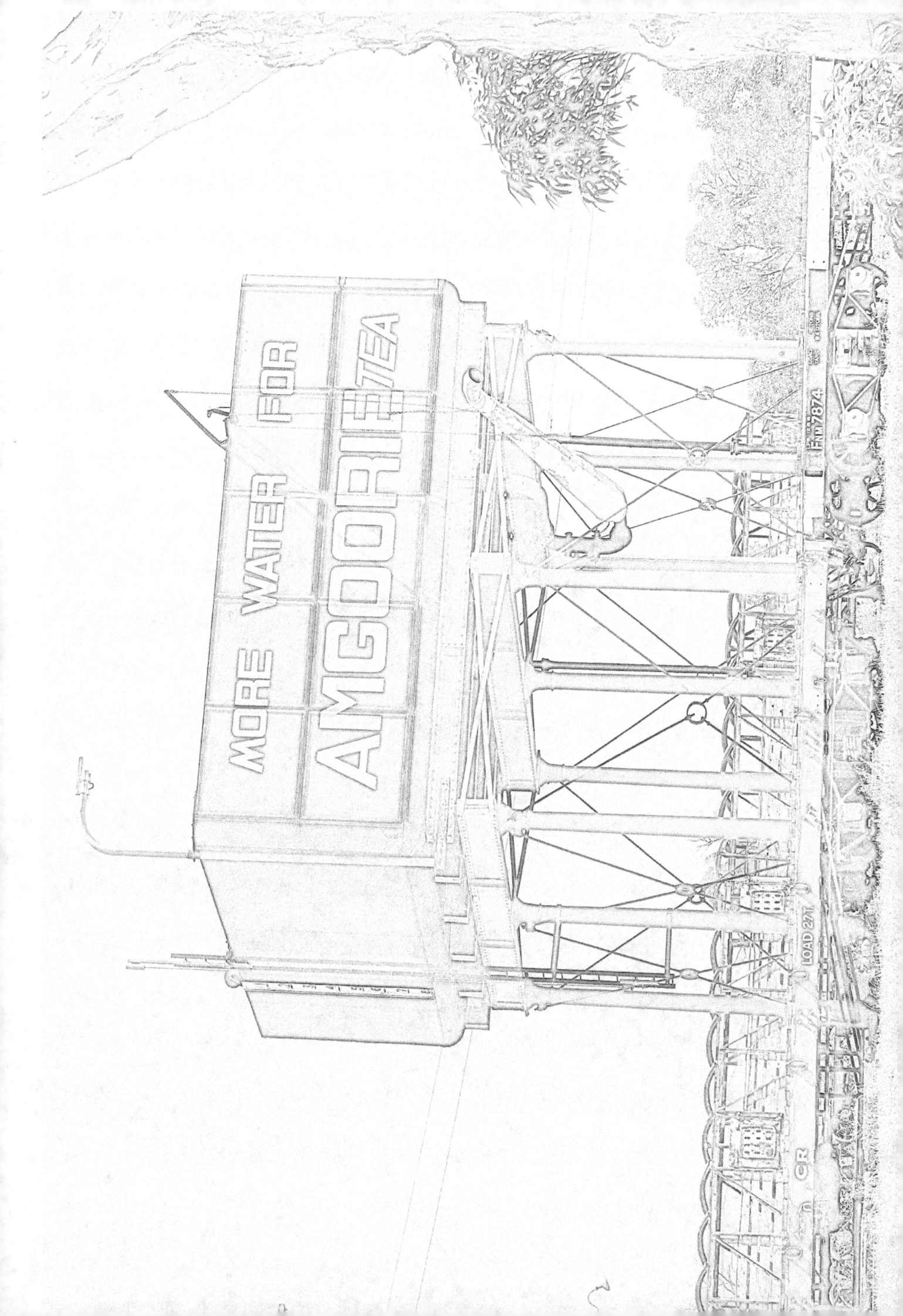

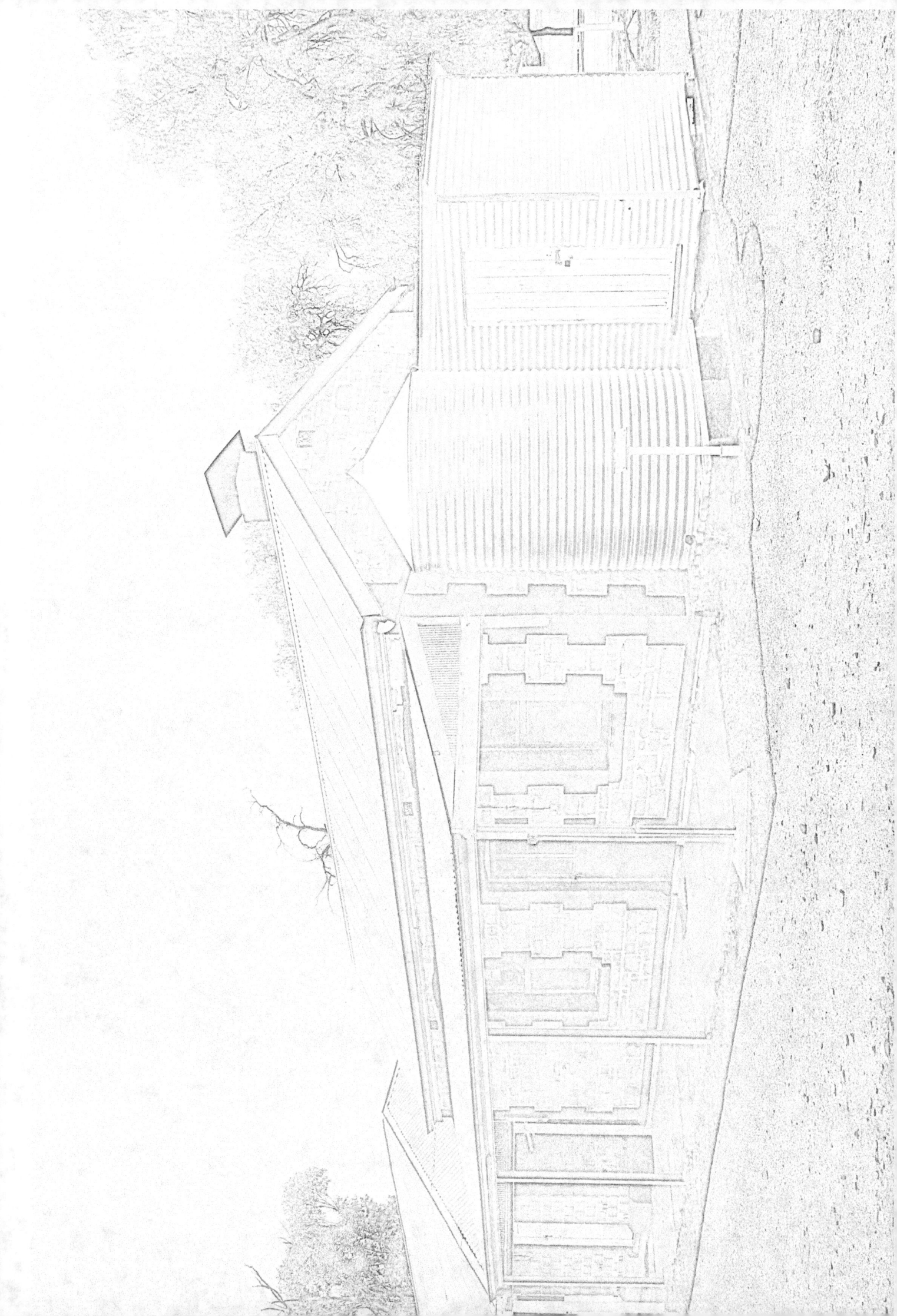